GOTHIC *and* STRANGE TRUE TALES OF THE CIVIL WAR

KEVEN McQUEEN

AMERICA
THROUGH
TIME

America Through Time®
An imprint of Sutton Publishing Inc.
www.through-time.com

First published 2025

ISBN 978-1-63499-569-6

Typeset in 10pt on 13pt Sabon
Printed and bound in England

Preface

Can anything more be said about the Civil War, the national tragedy that resulted in 600,000 soldiers' deaths, freed the slaves, and defined the difference between individual states' rights and federal law? Surprisingly, yes.

As an inveterate reader of old newspapers going as far back as the 1830s, I have found in these contemporary sources many strange nuggets of information about events leading up to the conflict, events during the war, and events afterward. I feel confident that even the most devoted Civil War buffs will find some material in this book surprising. For example:

Owning a slave sometimes led to unexpected legal complications not mentioned in standard history books.

One of Lincoln's assassins had ties to a man considered a suspect in England's Jack the Ripper murders twenty-three years later.

Most people think selling humans at auction ended with the Civil War; in fact, it was still legal for decades afterward and had the backing of the Constitution.

While most slaveowners were white, scores of wealthy antebellum blacks also owned slaves—some white, some black.

Everyone has seen Matthew Brady photos depicting fields covered with scores of dead soldiers. In the larger battles, fatalities could number in the tens of thousands. How were so many bodies disposed of in those days before heavy machinery? In many cases, the answer was: not very well.

It is well known that after Lincoln's death, his body was embalmed and taken on a funeral train through several states for mourners to see. But the full story is considerably more disturbing.

Civil War soldiers' bravery is justly celebrated, but we seldom read about the tricks some men employed to avoid service.

Except for general groupings within chapters, this book's information is not organized in any specific way, nor is there an overall theme except for the devastation brought by the war, the heroism of those who fought in it, and the strange side effects war has on society. Readers will find the usual historical facts—the date of a specific battle, the generals who fought, which side won—as byproducts of unusual historical stories.

If there is an overarching concept at all, it is the outré side of history—the gothic, the bizarre, the darkly humorous, occasionally even the supernatural. Perhaps the reader could consider perusing the book like strolling through a museum: stop and ponder a strange exhibit, then move on to the next one when the whim strikes.

Contents

Special Thanks

Stacy Barnes, city administrator of Greensburg, KS; Eastern Kentucky University Department of English; Eastern Kentucky University Interlibrary Loan Department; Denise and Amber Hughes; Amy Hawkins McQueen and Quentin Hawkins; Darrell and Swecia McQueen; Darren, Alison, Elizabeth, and Charles David McQueen; Kyle McQueen; Michael, Lori, and Blaine McQueen; Evan Holbrook and Calypso Rucker; Craig and Debbie Smith; Mia Temple; Alan Sutton, Josh Greenland, and everyone at Sutton Publishing/America Through Time. Also: The Father of Lights.

Check out my Facebook author page and my website, Kevenmcqueenstories.com.

1

The Legal Quandaries of Slave-owning

Not only did human beings owning others as slaves create ethical and moral dilemmas, it also created many legal ones: the sort that probably would not occur to the average modern person, and some of which decidedly backfired on the slaveholding system. Here are some of the more bizarre.

A slave was arrested in Boonville, Missouri, on charges of creating a false order for a merchant's goods. When the case went to trial in November 1842, Judge Morrow quashed the indictment by ruling that "a Negro could not commit forgery." The judge's reasoning was that since slaves were not recognized as persons under the law, they ipso facto could not commit crimes ("Novel Decision" 3).

In 1845, the governor of Virginia commuted the sentence of a slave who murdered his master from death to banishment to Canada. The *Louisville Journal* worried about the possible legal ramifications. "If this is to be the punishment of the crime, will not the killing of masters get to be the universal device of all slaves who wish to go to Canada?" ("A slave, convicted" 2).

Simon Porter, a free black, fell off a wagon at Scott County, Kentucky, and died of his injuries a few days later, on September 30, 1848. He owned a house and considerable property, and his wife and children were slaves. Said the baffled *Georgetown Herald*, "What disposition will be made of his estate, we are at a loss to divine; just such another case has never come under our observation" ("Simon Porter..." 1).

Julius Hawkins, a former slave, lived in Cincinnati and worked as a steward on the steamboat *Melodeon*. When the vessel docked at Louisville one day, he was seized by descendants of his former master "on a claim of balance due on the purchase of his freedom many years ago." Cutting through the legalese, they meant that Hawkins had not fully paid for his freedom, and they were determined to collect the rest of it. He was clapped in jail at Frankfort, Kentucky, until the law figured out what to do. In the meanwhile, his friends in Cincinnati raised $600 to purchase his liberty should it prove necessary. In March 1849, the judge decided that since Hawkins had been free for several years with his former master's best wishes, "the presumption in favor of his freedom being too strong to be resisted, and no law authorizing his detention or re-enslavement," the heirs could not collect. The *Cincinnati Chronicle* remarked, "We are very happy to record this decision by a Kentucky court; and, in doing so, we should do injustice ... if we did not add that nowhere in this broad Union are the rights of a colored man, asserting a legal claim to freedom, more sincerely respected or more effectively guaranteed, than by the judiciary and the public sentiment of Kentucky." In other words, when it came to contested questions of freedom, Bluegrass State courts generally did the right thing. And Julius vowed he would pay his former master's heirs that $150 he owed anyway, with interest ("Julius Hawkins" 2).

Other legal cans of worms were opened by persons of indeterminate race when the system was at a loss to decide whether they should be enslaved. Twenty-six-year-old Amanda Jane had been held in slavery since birth, but in October 1851, the circuit court of Rockingham County, Virginia, ruled after a weeklong trial that she was in fact white. Astonishingly, the court came to this decision even though Amanda's mother Sally was a slave. "The testimony proving her to be of Negro extraction was of the strongest and clearest kind," said a contemporary reporter, "And yet the appearance of the woman seemed to contradict it all" ("A White Woman Released from Slavery" 3).

Another case involved John Fletcher of Louisville. When his case went to trial on November 14, 1851, no one could tell whether he was black or Indian, slave or free. Naturally, Fletcher declared he was a free Indian. The court ruled that he was black and challenged him to prove otherwise within the next twenty-four hours and cough up $500 bail besides ("A Novel Trial" 3). He could not prove his contention, and the next day he was sold to a hotelkeeper for a year's servitude for fifty-six dollars ("Police Court" November 17, 1851 2).

Adam Wynne of Goldsboro, North Carolina, was a free black—but he owned his wife and several children, all of whom he had purchased. *Circa* March 1852, Wynne got into financial arrears and sold his family members for prices ranging from $711 to $827 ("Singular Sale of Slaves" 2).

Fred Harper of Louisville owned a slave named Andrew Martin, who was caught in the act of stealing glassware from a Mrs. Postlethwait's house on August 14, 1852. He was punished with thirty lashes of the whip—and then it was discovered that he was free. What was the law to do about this mistake? They couldn't exactly take back the whipping. So they sentenced him to extra "proper" punishment: a jury trial and a certain sentence in the penitentiary. Then things got even more complicated. Martin had been free, but recently he had sold himself into slavery to a Mr. Fred Harper, so he was a slave after all ("The Negro Martin" 3; "Another Slave Case" 3; "Police Court" August 16, 1852 3).

What to do now? The court ruled on August 16 that he was free anyway, no matter what he claimed, and since he already had been flogged, he would be released with no further penalty. They gave Andrew to Mr. Harper, evidently to let Harper puzzle out what to do with him ("Police Court" August 17, 1852 3).

Mr. Roane's slaves were up for sale in Bardstown, Kentucky, one day in the 1850s, against Roane's wishes. A later account explained that the slaves "were being forced into public auction by a man who owned a chattel mortgage on them" (Bories 1). The first woman on the auction block was a nurse who held the family's baby, Sally, as the bidding war started. Suddenly it dawned on Roane: the law held that "any child on the block with the slave when the sale was made went to the purchaser." Not only was Roane's slave for sale, so was his daughter! A huge predicament was avoided when one of Roane's friends made the winning bid and gave both little Sally and the nurse back to him. Technically, Mr. Roane owned his daughter, and abolitionists used the story as an illustration of the inherent absurdity of slavery (Bories 1). In 1938, when Sally Roane Wickliffe was an elderly woman living in Silver Hills, New Albany, Indiana, her adventure earned her a guest shot on the *Ripley's Believe It or Not* radio show ("C-J Feature" 2). She died on March 20, 1939 ("Woman, Sold as Baby..." 14).

In 1854, Hatcher and Gentry ran a tobacco factory in Richmond, Virginia, and employed two slaves. Gentry hired one of them to set fire to the place, presumably to collect insurance. Afterward the slave became a Christian and said God would never forgive him if he kept the dark secret. But since the laws of the state would not permit a slave to testify against whites, the man who induced him to commit arson could not be tried ("Two slaves employed..." 3).

A young man in Louisville bought an $8 lottery ticket and sold half of it to slave Jim Breckinridge on April 7, 1857. The ticket won, yielding the $30,000 prize. Jim was entitled to $12,750 after the state got its percentage ("[Negro] in Luck" 3). Modern equivalent: slightly over $400,000. But there was a legal issue. Did the money belong to Jim or could his owner, lawyer Isaac Green, claim it? The question never came up in court since Green relinquished any theoretical rights to the money. On April 8, Jim bought his own freedom for $600 (modern equivalent, about $19,000—a low price for an adult slave in 1857, so Green was generous in more ways than one). Jim also purchased and freed his wife and two children ("The Lucky Prize Freedom" 3).

An overseer named Davenport killed a slave in Vicksburg, Mississippi. Possibly to Davenport's surprise, he was arrested and tried in April 1858. He argued that he had killed the slave for "resisting his authority." We might assume an open and shut victory for Davenport in those unenlightened times, but Judge Verger opined that if a slave felt his life was threatened, he had the right to resist. The jury convicted Davenport for manslaughter and sentenced him to seven years' hard labor in the penitentiary ("Interesting to Slaveholders" 1).

Free black Reese purchased his wife and children from W. O. Smith in Louisville. But Smith died before the transaction could be completed, and his heirs refused to honor it. Reese filed a suit in circuit court. The case was heard on June 15, 1859, and the jury decided in his favor. The *Louisville Courier*, a proslavery paper, commented: "The verdict was consistent with the testimony, and proper and right" ("Reese Wins His Wife and Children" 1).

In the same year, another interesting predicament for the law came to light in Louisville. Saloonkeeper George Weston bought a slave woman from John Staniford for $52. (Modern equivalent about $1,720, and a cut-rate price for a slave. Perhaps Weston should have been suspicious.) Only after the purchase did Weston realize that she was insane. Weston swore out a felony warrant charging Staniford with fraud. The legal question, though not the moral question, was whether the woman was insane at the time of purchase or became so afterward; in the latter case, Weston would have no grounds for a lawsuit. Staniford's attorneys argued that even if the slave were crazy when purchased, it should be considered a mere breach of contract, not a felony, and thus a civil case, not a criminal one. Weston countered that all he wanted was his money back. To complicate the case further, some contended that the "slave" actually was free, and Weston sheepishly (I assume) admitted that the original bill of sale stated that the woman was not of sound mind, but he didn't read it thoroughly until after the sale, and also that he lost the document ("Selling a Crazy Negro" 1; "Sale of an Insane Negro" 1). It sounds as though Weston had a losing case, and also that he was the kind of guy who takes medicine without reading the directions first. Yet something must have been going on behind the scenes because Staniford compromised. He refunded the money and took back the crazy slave. In return, the judge discharged Staniford but left him with a warning: "The court gave both parties to understand that the woman must be removed from the city, as it was the too common custom of persons leaving their imbecile and broken down Negroes to the charities of the city and the general support of the public" ("The Negro Case" 1). So, presumably, she ended up in an asylum. In a somewhat similar Louisville case, a con artist named Keats was arrested on May 3, 1861, for selling an already-mortgaged slave to a Mrs. Comstock ("Arrested on a Felony Warrant" 4).

Joe Perry was a well-to-do free black living in Winchester, Kentucky. When he decided to take unto himself a wife, he bought one. Sometime after the honeymoon, Perry decided he didn't want to be married after all and should sell his slave-wife. He dropped her off in Lexington in March 1860 to be delivered to the auction block. No doubt this might have created a legal dilemma, but he confided his plan to some friends in town who thought it "a violation of all the laws of gallantry and human nature," as the *Covington Democrat* phrased it. A few days later they went to Winchester, seized Joe, tied him to a tree, and beat him until he changed his mind. He hurried back to Lexington and gathered his wife before she was sold ("Cupidity Versus Cupid" 1).

On Christmas Day 1860, two slaves fought over 10 cents in a grocery near Louisville. Mr. W. D. Tinsley's John fatally stabbed Mr. Jacob Smyser's John in the arteries of his right arm and left thigh ("Inquest No. 248" 1; "Murder for Ten Cents" 1; "In Jail" 1). It was not uncommon for one slave to murder another, and it almost always led to legal difficulties. The outcome in this instance was remarkable: on New Year's Day 1861, the police court ruled that the killing was self-defense. There was not sufficient proof that the one John had intentionally murdered the other, yet in Kentucky slaves could not be punished for manslaughter ("The slave John..." 1; "John, a slave..." 1). So Tinsley's John walked from the courthouse free in one sense, yet not in another.

In 1857, a Missourian bequeathed in his will $500 to ten slaves, but only on the condition that they move to Liberia or someplace "set apart for free persons." The slaves chose to stay in Missouri, but since they did not move as required in the terms of the will, they did not get the money. Ten years later, the St. Louis County Court ruled that since slavery had since been abolished in the USA, the former slaves were now living in a "country set apart for free persons." They each got their $500 ("A curious case is reported from Missouri..." 1).

Yet another tangle had to be extricated after the war: were slave marriages contracted before freedom to be considered legally binding? It had to be decided after Solomon McReynolds of Montgomery County, Tennessee, was convicted of bigamy when he married for a second time after emancipation though his first wife, whom he had wedded while they were both slaves, was still alive. The Supreme Court ruled on April 27, 1868, that "marriages contracted during slavery were not valid, unless the parties contracting remained together after their emancipation" ("Negro Marriages" 1). The first Mrs. McReynolds's thoughts on the decision are not recorded.

2

A Miscellany of Strange Incidents

The Battle of Big Hill in Kentucky wasn't exactly a tide-turner. Fought on August 23, 1862, on a mountain where Madison, Jackson, and Rockcastle Counties meet, it resulted in the deaths of a few Confederates. It is remembered as a minor skirmish leading up to the larger Battle of Richmond in Madison County a week later. However, Big Hill had a virtually unknown—and unpleasantly porcine—sequel.

There was a long forgotten second Battle of Big Hill. Several weeks after the first one, unsubstantiated reports alleged that on October 15, Kirby Smith's Confederate army was trying to retake Big Hill and that they had been "badly whipped" by General Thomas ("It is rumored..." 3; "Richmond Battle at Big Hill" 3). The *Louisville Journal* scoffed, stating on October 18 that it had "received no confirmation of the exciting rumors. On the contrary, it is the belief of the military authorities here that no such collision took place," and pointing out that their correspondent at nearby Stanford had not heard of it ("The Rumored Fight at Big Hill" 1).

Corroboration came two days later. Union soldiers had in fact killed more of the enemy on Big Hill, with help from civilians. Loyalist mountaineers had felled trees to block roads, impeding the Confederates' escape, and had gone after them with shotguns ("We are informed by a correspondent..." 3). How many were slain? The papers didn't say, and we may never know since hogs ate the bodies. The *Journal* chortled editorially on October 24, "We don't think we shall buy our winter's pork from that section" ("Such of the hogs as are left..." 2). Two weeks later one of the newspaper's correspondents, J. G. George, hooted at the soldiers' grim fate: "Madison County fat hogs are on the move in this direction—*fat as corn and dead rebels could make them.* Want to buy?" (George 3).

Today, there is a small cemetery at Big Hill with thirteen military headstones for the Confederates who died there. Eight are dated August 1862, five are undated. Perhaps those five were the ones killed at the same location in October—assuming that after the hogs got done with them, there were enough remains to commemorate.

The Battle of Painter Creek wasn't the sort of encounter that is commemorated in history books or by reenactors or becomes the subject of stirring books or movies. It started out excitingly. A large Confederate force led by Colonel Joseph Porter engaged in a fight against several Union regiments headed by General John McNeil near Macon,

The Confederate cemetery at Big Hill, KY. It appears some of the dead soldiers were eaten by hogs. (*Photo by author*)

Missouri, on August 8, 1862. Porter and McNeil had already clashed at Kirksville on August 6, and many rebels were killed or captured. Porter retreated southward into the woods. McNeil was determined to pursue and capture him, hence the clash at Painter Creek when the forces met again.

The Union soldiers took position on high knobs and rained fire down on the Confederates. Porter's men fired back, refusing to budge. In the opinion of Charley Coleman, a civilian witness, Porter could have driven off the Federals but was overly cautious because he had panic-stricken new recruits in his regiment.

The two sides traded heavy fire for hours. Said Coleman years later: "From the terrific discharges of musketry we [civilian eyewitnesses] imagined the ground must have been covered with the slain. I didn't see how human flesh and blood could last a minute under such a riot of smoke and fire."

At dusk, the knobs echoed with the sound of a Union bugler. The Northerners were on the retreat. Civilians steeled themselves to commence the grim task of burying the hundreds of dead soldiers they imagined must be littering the field. When they arrived, they found that despite the ferocious firing, nobody on either side had been injured or killed, though it wasn't from a lack of trying. The only corpse was a Confederate raw recruit who had jumped off his horse before the battle started and drowned in a creek.

The Battle of Painter Creek had been such a yawner that even during the height of the conflict, teacher Lizzie McKittrick insisted that her students keep at their lessons even though the sound and the fury of the conflict were audible ("Not One Hurt..." 4).

Union General John McNeil, who fought at the remarkably irrelevant Battle of Painter Creek, MO. (*Library of Congress Prints and Photographs Division*)

The violence of battle had an interesting effect on the local fauna: it sometimes made wild animals as tame as house pets. At the Battle of Stones River in Tennessee, soldiers observed that turkeys were so terrified by the noise that they sought to hide among men. Rabbits too were so "tamed by fright" that they sought protection under soldiers' coats ("A Singular Spectacle in Battle" 1).

At the Battle of Resaca, Georgia, in May 1864, a shell exploded with a loud whistle not far from where Confederate Generals Johnston and Polk were standing. After the explosion, witnesses heard a similar sound coming from somewhere overhead. They found a mockingbird perched in a tree calmly doing what mockingbirds do best: imitating the noise it had just heard ("The Mockingbird of Resaca" 3).

As Surgeon Mandeville of Boston operated under a tree at Bermuda Hundred, Virginia, on July 5, 1864, he was amazed to hear a carefree catbird entertaining soldiers with its lovely warble, although only ten feet away cannon were being reloaded and fired with abandon ("A Brave Bird..." 3).

When Booth performed his athletic leap onto the stage after shooting Lincoln, he brandished a knife before startled actor Harry Hawk and exclaimed Virginia's state motto, the Latin phrase "Sic semper tyrannis!"

At the assassins' trial in June, part of the testimony was kept out of the press. However, this alleged exchange did get leaked, possibly because someone considered it too good to remain secret: the judge asked a Ford's Theatre witness named Murphy, presumably an Irishman, if he had clearly heard what Booth shouted. "All he said," replied Murphy, "was 'I'm sick, send for McGinnis'" ("Secret Testimony" 1).

Loyal Confederate Mrs. Eugenia Philips of occupied New Orleans had a good, loud public chuckle on that day in May 1862. Who knows what she was laughing at? Perhaps she was thinking of a rib tickler from the latest edition of *Joe Miller's Joke Book*, or maybe she saw a hostler getting kicked in a mudhole by a prize-winning mule. She always claimed that she was laughing at her children's adorable antics. But a funeral train of deceased Union officers happened to be passing at the moment, and it was widely assumed she thought that was the object of her amusement. When Union Major General Benjamin Butler heard about it, he had her banished to Ship Island, Mississippi, on the legally questionable grounds of "unpatriotic levity" (Garrison *More Civil War* 14). She left the city to begin her exile on June 30 with a female servant. On her way out she said to Butler, "It has one advantage over the city, sir; you will not be there." It wasn't for nothing that contemporaneous New Orleanians produced chamber pots with a portrait of Butler at the bottom. On September 11, 1862, Mrs. Phillips was allowed to return home after reluctantly taking an oath of loyalty to the United States ("Eugenia Philips").

Circa August 1864, a writer for the *Jefferson County* (New York) *Union* estimated, among other wholesome matters, how much blood had been spilled thus far in the conflict. His statistics:

> If the dead were stretched out in one continuous line, the bodies would circle the state of New York.
>
> If these dead were encoffined and the caskets stacked like cordwood, there would be 39,000 cords.
>
> If placed in a wall, like building material and said wall were twenty-five feet thick and thirty feet high, the military casualties so far would make a wall over a mile-and-a-quarter long.
>
> Conversely, if the wall were only five feet thick and ten feet high, this barricade of the gone away would extend all the way across New York.
>
> If the soldiers were simply placed on the ground and not stacked in orderly fashion, they would cover every inch of ground in Jefferson County, probably making the place uninhabitable.

And, he added, 75,000 tons of human blood had been shed ("Seventy-Five Thousand Tons..." 1). I have no idea how he came to these calculations and assume that he was counting only dead Yankee soldiers, otherwise the numbers might have been even higher.

Who knows why? But while near Richmond, Virginia, just before February 20, 1862, a science-minded Union soldier whom one might suppose had bigger things on his mind caught what he must have considered an interesting looking lizard and sent it to Harvard's Museum of Comparative Zoology. The preserved specimen of *Aspidoscelis sexlineata sexlineata* is still there, known as exhibit MCZ-570 (Garrison *Civil War Curiosities* 82; "MCZ Herpetology R-570").

As a dead and presumably nasally offensive mule was dragged off the field at the Second Battle of Memphis in April 1864, a suspicious soldier gave it an exploratory bayonet stab. The carcass was stuffed with 60,000 percussion caps, ammunition, and other contraband articles, all stuffed within by a rebel smuggler ("A dead mule..." 3).

Many years after the war, Captain J. E. Elgin, formerly one of Confederate General John Hunt Morgan's men and by then living in Louisville, reminisced about what he considered "the most terrible exhibition of barbaric cruelty" he had witnessed during his time in the service. He reported regretfully that the perpetrator was a fellow Confederate.

Elgin had been placed in charge of one of the hospital corps after the Battle of Richmond, Kentucky. As he approached the line of the Federal wounded, he heard a man crying, "For God's sake, doctor, kill me! Don't cut off my legs and leave me a cripple for life!" Elgin saw that the alarmed soldier was tied to a log and had only a minor flesh wound in the thigh—yet the surgeon, a recent graduate from medical school, was determined to amputate his left leg, not out of incompetence but to render the soldier useless for further military service. He already had applied a tourniquet and was tracing the area he intended to cut with a knife blade. Elgin immediately arrested the surgeon and took him to Morgan and his second-in-command, Basil Duke.

The surgeon was court-martialed and sentenced to death by firing squad, yet somehow, he dodged this fate. Elgin speculated that some highly placed connection got him off. Nevertheless, he was cashiered out of the army.

Who was this brute of a doctor, and whatever happened to him? Elgin dropped some hints. The hater of the Union made his way North and settled in Reading, Pennsylvania, where he currently was a doctor—hopefully, one who now took the Hippocratic oath more seriously. At some point his allegiance had done a complete turnabout, and by 1892, the year Elgin told his story, he had transmogrified into "the rankest hater of the South, perhaps, in the state of Pennsylvania" ("A War Story about John Morgan..." 4).

Horses were as common as cannonballs during the war, but somehow Company B of the 43rd Mississippi Regiment procured a camel named Douglas. So distinctive was the animal that the company became known as the Camel Regiment. It was certainly handy at carrying officers' baggage and could go extended periods without drinking, but the downside was that horses were so afraid of it that its driver was ordered to keep it outside camp. But at Iuka, *en route* to the Battle of Corinth held from April 29 to May 30, 1862, the camel escaped. The regiment's horses stampeded in panic and injured several soldiers. A Minié ball ended the camel's military career on June 27, 1863, during the siege of Vicksburg (Garrison *Civil War Curiosities* 82; Bell passim).

Union General William King Kimball of the 12th Maine Volunteer Infantry Regiment committed suicide on September 2, 1875. He left a note to the coroner with a striking military analogy: "I go to the front as a volunteer, not waiting to be drafted by the grim messenger" ("Gen. W.K. Kimball..." 3).

William H. Ledsome, an old soldier of Parkersburg, West Virginia, wished to be prepared for that coming day when the angel Gabriel blows his horn and the dead shall rise. Just before he passed away in November 1909, he ordered that he be buried in a robe with two large wings sewed to it. At his funeral, it was found that the wings were missing. Ledsome's son-in-law postponed the ceremony until they were replaced ("Buried with Wings" 3).

Which Confederate soldiers are buried farthest from home? Likely candidates include the 139 rebels who rest in Oakwood Cemetery near Madison, Wisconsin. One hundred and ten of them were from the 1st Alabama. They died of illness at Camp Randall in 1861. Not long after the war's conclusion, Alice Waterman of Baton Rouge moved to Madison; she made it her hobby and pleasure to tend to the graves of the Southerners.

She personally pulled up weeds, had their names painted on headboards, and paid for a stone border around their resting places. When Mrs. Waterman died on September 15, 1897, she had the unusual honor of being buried among the long-dead Confederates ("Woman in a Soldier Cemetery" 7).

At the Second Battle of Reams Station, Virginia, on August 25, 1864, Confederate Captain Shade Wooten of North Carolina escaped death three times by the simple expedient of throwing dirt in the eyes of Union soldiers who were aiming at him (Garrison *More Civil War* 122).

The feared Missouri Confederate guerrilla William Quantrill was shot by Federal troops near Taylorsville, Kentucky, on May 10, 1865, and died nearly a month later in a Louisville prison hospital on June 6. He was buried in an unmarked grave in the city's Portland Catholic cemetery.

One intriguing facet of human psychology is the refusal to admit that the dead—whether heroes or villains—are truly dead. Often, when a significant figure dies, rumor has it that he is alive and in hiding, or a lookalike died in his place as part of a conspiracy. It was said of Nero, King Arthur, James Dean, JFK and Lee Harvey Oswald, John Wilkes Booth, Glenn Miller, Jesse James, Billy the Kid, Andy Kaufman, Elvis, Hitler, John Dillinger, Jim Morrison, and (after a fashion) Walt Disney.

The same rumor attached to Quantrill. As early as November 1865, those who admired or feared him claimed he wasn't really dead. On December 2, the *Louisville Journal*—a newspaper located in the city where Quantrill died—reported as fact that he was headed for D.C. to obtain a pardon ("The horrid wretch" 2). In March 1866, the same paper reported that he was living in Mexico ("Quantrell [*sic*], the Missouri guerrilla"). Only two days later, the *Journal* stated that Quantrill had been positively identified in New York by Kansas's Senator Lane ("Identification of Guerrilla" 4).

Just a week later, the *New York Tribune* stated authoritatively that Quantrill was in prison in D.C., where nearly 100 witnesses agreed that it was he ("Guerrilla Quantrell [*sic*] in Washington" 4). "[I]t is supposed a mistake in his identification will be impossible," mused the paper. But it was possible, because the prisoner turned out to be Mr. W.L. Hamilton ("A Washington dispatch…" 3).

A week after that, Quantrill was said to be farming in Cuba ("A correspondent states…" 4). One might think that the public would be suspicious by then, but Quantrill-is-alive stories cropped up in the nation's papers for decades. As late as 1907, he was rumored to be living under the name John Sharp at Quatsino, Vancouver ("Denies Quantrill is Still Living" 4). The confusion lasted even after Quantrill's bones had been disinterred in 1887.

In that year, Quantrill's mother requested to have her infamous son's bones exhumed and moved to a family cemetery. She hired family friend William G. Scott, who turned out not to be to such a friend after all. Rather than doing his job, he tried to sell Quantrill's skull and various pieces of his arm and leg bones to collectors. The market for the remains was not as bullish as Scott expected, however, so Quantrill's limbs ended up on the Kansas State Historical Society at Topeka. The Dover (Delaware) Historical Society owns Quantrill's head (Garrison *More Civil War* 56). His mother had the rest of the remains buried beside his father in Canal Dover, Ohio ("Quantrill's Body Rests in Ohio…" 8).

3
Tough Soldiers

On May 25, 1862, at the First Battle of Winchester, Virginia, a soldier of the 21st North Carolina received two Minié ball wounds in his thighs (shot from opposite directions); another near the elbow, which ventured up his arm and exited at the clavicle; and a third in the small of his back. Surgeons were unable to locate this third bullet, but several days later the soldier "passed it." As he would pass digested food, that is. "No parallel case on record!" said the doctors. A Dr. Chapel found this so amazing that he kept the slightly flattened bullet as a souvenir. As for the soldier, although he was still an inmate of the Seminary hospital in Winchester in early July, he was reportedly eating heartily, clear-eyed and cheerful, and nearly healed of all his horrific wounds ("A Curious Set of Wounds" 3).

In November 1863, a war correspondent using the pen name "Old Soldier" related what he considered a rib-tickling event at Shiloh: "An orderly riding past me ... was struck by a cannonball, which cut him in two pieces." The bisected man lived just long enough to say in a tone of great surprise, "Look here, will you!" Old Soldier recalled, "I couldn't help laughing then, and I laugh now every time I think of the incident. He suffered no pain and died as every soldier would wish to die, at his post" ("Wounded" 1).

A *New York Sun* correspondent chanced to see a veteran in February 1864 who was missing his left hand. "How did that happen?" asked the nosey journalist. The wounded man, who obviously shared an all-encompassing sense of humor with Old Soldier, as noted above, enjoyed "a hearty laugh" and replied, "I lost that hand under such funny circumstances that I can't help laughing every time I think of it!" Then he explained that while in the service he sometimes did barbering on the side. One day the sergeant asked for a shave. The soldier applied lather and shaved both of the sergeant's cheeks and was just tilting the latter's head to scrape off his beard when a shell removed both the soldier's hand and the sergeant's head. The vet used onomatopoeic sound effects to enhance the scene: "Whiff! Bang!"

"Where they went I never knew," he guffawed. "I didn't set eyes on either of them afterwards, but every time I think of it, I can't help laughing!"

Immediately after his maiming, the soldier laughed so hard at the wholesome humor in the situation that the surgeon in attendance lost his temper and threatened to leave him to his own devices if he didn't comport himself with decorum. And when the soldier got back to camp, his comrades also found the incident hilarious—perhaps they didn't like the sergeant—and joshed him by exclaiming that no way were they going to let him give them a shave. While hearing this tale, the journalist chuckled too, as did passersby who "laughed to see the soldier so happy" ("A Volunteer Shave" 4). Maybe you just had to be there.

A Yankee lieutenant who had lost a leg in North Carolina donned a prosthetic and fought in the Battle of Olustee, Florida, on February 20, 1864. A Confederate sharpshooter shot him through the wooden leg, which the lieutenant considered just the last word in funny. He left battle to find his colonel, to whom he announced, "Devilish good joke on the fellows!" Then he hopped his way back to whence he came and continued where he left off ("A lieutenant at the late battle..." 4).

A sixteen-year-old soldier shot through the brain in western Louisiana in May 1864 revived long enough to favor the surgeons with a verse from the song "Do They Miss Me at Home?" Then his singing ended for all time ("A late New Orleans paper says..." 4).

One wonders if Matthew Phenix of Company B, 86th New York volunteers, was aware of his mythological namesake, a creature which never can be destroyed. On November 27, 1863, a foreign body entered his left eye at the Battle of Mine Run, Virginia. He didn't get medical care until he was sent to the Baptist Church hospital at Alexandria on December 4. Dr. C. P. Bigelow probed the wound—repeatedly, undoubtedly with sound effects quite appropriate to a Three Stooges short—but could not find the metal. In May 1864, after yet more plundering, the surgeon found the wayward chunk. He dug around with his forceps but could not get a grip on it. But the next day, success! The obstruction had changed its position enough that Dr. Bigelow could grasp it and pull it out. It turned out not to be a mere bullet after all, but an iron grapeshot 1.5 inches in diameter ("A

Nurse Anna Bell Stubbs treats wounded soldiers at No. 1 Nashville Hospital. Like most Civil War nurses, she was very busy. (*Library of Congress Prints and Photographs Division*)

Remarkable Case" 3). In other words, Phenix had strolled the earth five months with a half-pound small cannonball in his head.

A Northern soldier who was shot at the Battle of Yellow Tavern, Virginia, on May 11, 1864, survived long enough to write his last will and testament: "I, John Wilheimer, Second New York Cavalry, am shot and dying. Whoever finds me, send this to Sarah Wilheimer, Brooklyn post office, New York. She is my sister and only relative in the country. Oh, my poor sister! Do not break your heart; but I am shot through the breast and dying, and they have gone and left me here. [Passage obscured by bloodstain.] Write to Conrad Vitmare of our company; he owes me fifty dollars, which he will pay you. Oh, my dear sister, farewell!"

The Southerners forwarded the letter to Sarah under a flag of truce ("A Last Will and Testament" 1).

During Louisiana's protracted Battle of Port Hudson, Confederate Captain R. M. Boone's leg was blown off by Union artillery. Knowing he would bleed to death shortly, his dying request was that his amputated limb be shot back at the enemy via cannon (Garrison *More Civil War* 51).

In 1864, a Massachusetts sergeant required amputation of his hand. A surgeon offered chloroform. The sarge refused, saying, "If cutting is to be done on me, I want to see it." He laid his arm on the table, and the hand was removed without so much as a noise from the patient, though some observed that he gritted his teeth throughout the ordeal. The impressed surgeon remarked, "You ought to have been a surgeon, my man!"

"I was the next thing to one afore I enlisted," replied the just-modified sergeant.

"What was that?"

"A butcher!" ("An 'Off-Hand' Joke" 1).

One of the war's many wounded: Richard D. Dunphy, formerly coal heaver of U.S. Navy. He was awarded the Congressional Medal of Honor. (*Library of Congress Prints and Photographs Division*)

Calvin Aldus of Belfast, Maine, was a member of the 7th Maine Regiment which attacked the rebel fortifications near Petersburg, Virginia, in June 1864. He was shot fifteen times through his clothing and emerged without a scratch. His luck could only hold out so long. As he approached a breastwork, a bullet hit him in the head and knocked him unconscious. After a while, the Confederates noticed that he was moving and opened fire. Aldus was shot in the shoulder, in the side, and through the thigh, and received four additional wounds. The tide of battle turned; as the victorious North moved forward, a retreating Confederate saw that Aldus was not dead and walloped him over the head with a musket. Aldus's comrades took him for dead, but at last he was revived and was sent to a hospital at Augusta in his home state for recuperation. One morning he was missing. He had sneaked away and forged a pass and later was located in Baltimore. He wanted to return to the front ("A Miraculous Escape" 1)!

In January 1865, a war correspondent told the tale of a mortally wounded, but thrifty, officer from New England who was determined to get a final bargain, arguing with an embalmer who usually charged $90 to preserve an officer. The dying man was pleased that he talked the mortician down to $87.50, thus saving $2.50 as his final act ("The Yankee Passion Strong in Death" 4).

During the siege of Richmond, Virginia, on July 28, 1864, the 19th Alabama suffered heavy losses. The regiment's color bearer was shot down as he hoisted the flag. So was his replacement, then another, until six had died. A seventh grabbed the flag and planted it on the Northerners' breastworks just as a bullet ended his life. The enemy was impressed with his courage in the face of impossible odds and buried him with a marker that read, "Here lies the color bearer of the Nineteenth Alabama Regiment. He was a brave soldier and planted his colors upon our works; may he rest in peace" ("A Tribute to Gallantry" 1).

Confederate Colonel (later Major General) John Brown Gordon got a hole shot through his hat at Antietam on September 17, 1862, with no injury to himself. Later in the day, a Yankee bullet entered his face—the fifth wound he received that day, not counting the damage to his hat. Gordon might have drowned in his blood if not for the previously made hole in his cap, which allowed it to drain away (Garrison *Civil War Curiosities* 92).

Captain George Biddulph of Company K, 36th Illinois Volunteers, was wounded at the Battle of Franklin, Tennessee, on November 30, 1864—just how badly no one knew at first. Something hit him in the head, blinding his left eye, deafening his left ear, and fracturing his jaw. He assumed it was a piece of a shell. Whatever it was, it left a sizable hole on the left side of his nose. The projectile had even turned, split one tooth in half, and turned another halfway around in its socket. Biddulph was sent home afterward.

He got an unexpected Christmas gift on December 25, 1866, when he felt a strange sensation in his head, after which his hearing was restored. A month later, on January 26, 1867, the veteran felt a severe pain in his throat. After he coughed up blood for a while, out came a bullet weighing an ounce. It was over an inch long and three-fourths of an inch wide. And it wasn't smooth, either; it was "ragged as cinders from the furnace." Doctors determined that it had been hiding all the while behind Biddulph's throat, about an inch below the palate ("A Strange Account of the Effect..." 3).

But at least Biddulph got rid of his unwanted companion. Another soldier, nineteen-year-old Ole Eversen of Company K, 2nd Wisconsin Infantry, took a rifle bullet in the brain at the First Battle of Bull Run. There it remained after surgeons decided it was too dangerous to remove. Eversen was reported in March 1867 to be a healthy farmer with no worse effects from his injury than the occasional headache ("A Man Carries a Bull Run Bullet..." 1).

Illustration depicting the search for wounded by torchlight. (*Library of Congress Prints and Photographs Division*)

Confederate killed by a shell fragment to the head at Petersburg, VA. (*Library of Congress Prints and Photographs Division*)

Union soldier Abraham De Bord of Washington County, Kentucky, was shot in the forehead in a skirmish at Fair Garden, Tennessee, on January 27, 1864. He had what seemed to be an exit wound on his temple, leading bystanders to believe that the Minié ball had passed right through his head and that De Bord was dead. They were wrong on both counts. He revived after a while and was shipped home. The wound did not heal, and De Bord was afflicted with several years' worth of headaches and a constant discharge dripping from the holes in his head. Yet his intelligence and thought processes did not seem affected. In June 1870, Louisville physicians examined De Bord and while trephining their patient's head found that the bullet was still in his brain. They theorized that what seemed to be an exit wound was caused by a fragment of the ball chipping off. De Bord made a speedy recovery after surgery ("A Singular Case" 4).

Confederate soldier James G. Marston of the 4th Louisiana was wounded at Atlanta on July 28, 1864. How badly wounded, he never knew. After he died in Clinton on June 19, 1870, a postmortem showed that he had been carrying a bullet in his brain all the time ("The *Clinton* [LA] *Patriot* describes..." 2).

Major Moderwell of Geneseo, Illinois, was shot in the stomach in Tennessee. The bullet carried along a gold pen and a fragment of a silver pen case. In March 1872, Moderwell went to the doctor for treatment of what he thought was a boil on his neck. It turned out to be a quarter inch-wide piece of the gold pen ("Major Moderwell..." 3).

An unnamed Georgia Confederate's nose was sliced off by a saber in the heat of battle. Rather than do without it, he put the nose back on his face and tied a cloth around his head to hold it in place in hopes that it would "take root" and stay there. It did, but the soldier was unaware that he put it on upside down. We are assured by the contemporary press that "when he wants to blow his nose he is compelled to stand on his head." That was probably a dark little joke, but the man with the inverted proboscis exhibited himself at the Macon Fair in autumn 1873 ("Savannah..." 2).

Consider the military career of William H. Brown, a private in the 18th Iowa Infantry, who survived a litany of grotesque injuries. He enlisted at Sigourney in August 1862, and everything went downhill after that. First, he was wounded by a shell at the Second Battle of Springfield, Missouri, on January 8, 1863. Then he was shot in the side at the Battle of Poison Spring in Arkansas, April 18, 1864.

He got through the battles of Prairie D'Ane and Jenkins' Ferry unscathed, but then Brown and four fellow soldiers were captured by the guerrilla Quantrill. His comrades were all killed, but Brown survived fifteen bullet wounds, including one that entered above his right eye and lodged in his brain; another directly through the right eye, which remained under his ear; another under the left eye (that bullet was successfully removed); another in the left side of the neck, which took up permanent residence near Brown's windpipe; another that traveled under the right arm and through his lungs, exiting under his left arm; one under each hip; five in the right thigh, which shattered his kneecap; and two in the left thigh which could not be removed. That leaves one more wound, the location of which journalists did not account for. Of the fifteen bullets, nearly all remained where Quantrill's men left them.

Brown visited relatives in St. Louis in May 1867. A reporter described him thus: "His face is not so badly disfigured as to make him all ugly, while with the aid of a crutch and cane he is able to go about, yet in a crippled condition." But at least he was "cheerful in conversation and takes his fate like a philosopher" ("The Tenacity of Life" 3).

William Quantrill. His men shot Pvt. William Brown fifteen times, yet Brown survived. (*Library of Congress Prints and Photographs Division*)

Michael Head, a former soldier working as a grocery clerk in Edgefield, Tennessee, was washing his face one day in April 1875 when a battered Minié ball popped out of his mouth. It had been lodged in Head's head since the Battle of Pine Mountain, eleven years before. He was "very much astonished," said a reporter ("*Nashville Banner*" 2).

General William Bolton of the 51st Pennsylvania Volunteers got an irremovable bullet in the back of the neck when the Union exploded a tunnel under the Confederate camp at Petersburg, Virginia, on July 30, 1864. In fact, no one shot him; when a Confederate canister shell blew up, it sent the bullet right into the same spot where Bolton had been wounded at Antietam. Doctors made forty incisions but could not remove the bullet. However, in May 1881, nature did what doctors couldn't. Bolton, by then a storekeeper living in Norristown, went on a coughing jag in front of a customer. Out came a quantity of blood and a rust-covered, sharp-edged bullet ("Coughing Up a Bullet" 1).

A similar incident befell veteran August Sutherland of Lynn, Massachusetts, who on March 23, 1894, coughed out an unpleasant souvenir he had received at the Battle of Culpeper Court House, Virginia, in September 1863. Surprisingly, Sutherland was unaware that he had been shot in the neck and thought his pains were caused by throat cancer ("A Bullet in His Neck" 7).

Confederate George Nichol of Franklin, Tennessee, was shot twice in the head. One bullet hit him in the mouth and the other entered his right eye. The latter missile lay dormant until October 1870, when it fell out of Nichol's mouth as he was laughing ("The *Franklin*...." 2).

Captain J. R. McConnell carried a war bullet in his head for decades. By August 1891, McConnell worked at the General Land Office in Washington, D.C. One day, he bent over to pick something up and it dropped harmlessly out of his nose. He kept the missile in his vest pocket thereafter ("A Curious Experience" 4).

Then there is the case of former Confederate Richard H. Scott, a tailor postbellum in Petersburg, Virginia. The bullet that entered him was never extracted. That fact preyed on his mind so badly that he committed suicide around New Year's Day 1870 ("Richard H. Scott..." 2).

4
The Executed

Some Civil War soldiers died in battle; many more died from disease. Others were responsible for their own untimely demises via court-martial and execution for offenses such as desertion, spying, treason, abusing civilians, and murder.

The first military execution in Kentucky resulted from the 1st and 2nd Kentucky Regiments being stationed on Union supporter William Sutherland's farm near Bardstown. On January 22, 1862, Sutherland found that two soldiers from the 2nd had killed a hog. He complained to Adjutant M. C. Brayles and Lieutenant Colonel Ruckstuhl, who immediately arrested and confined the soldiers, one unnamed by the press and the other, Private Samuel Calhoun from Company A, 2nd Regiment. The superior officers ordered the privates to drag the carcass with them.

Early the next morning, a soldier came to Sutherland's house and told a servant to ask the farmer to return to camp to receive payment for his butchered livestock. The physically feeble, sixty-seven-year-old—and too trusting—Sutherland accompanied the soldier. His son found him shot through the back four hundred yards from his home a few hours later ("Homicide Near Bardstown" 3).

It did not take military authorities long to conclude that Private Calhoun was guilty, especially since he had loudly sworn revenge against the farmer who had had the temerity to expose him. The killer was summarily court-martialed. During the trial, the other pig-slaughterer testified that Calhoun had confessed to him. Calhoun was found guilty on January 31. He admitted guilt again, this time to the 2nd Kentucky's chaplain. In fact, he acknowledged committing several hitherto undetected murders and additional manslaughters ("Court-Martial for Murder" 3). The military wasted no time hanging him on a strangely warm February 5.

A soldier who signed his communication "W.C." described the execution, which he called "the grandest and saddest scene of my life" to a newspaper. Evidently the military wanted to make an example of Calhoun to anyone else tempted to rob and kill a civilian. The hanging was held on the parade ground and attended by eight infantry regiments and two cavalry regiments, eight thousand men in all, including soldiers from the 35th Indiana. "His former comrades were marched out to look upon the end of him whose career might have been so honorable to himself and useful to his country," wrote the witness. Calhoun calmly prayed, waved to his buddies, and placed the cap over his head.

The end came at precisely 2:30 p.m. The assembled soldiers drilled afterward, but W.C. noticed that their hearts weren't in it ("Bruce's Brigade" 2; "Military Execution" 2).

Calhoun's brief life of crime, and his expiation for it, must have impressed onlookers, since Captain Green of the 35th Indiana announced plans to write his biography ("Captain Green..." 3).

Six isolated graves at the Confederate prison camp at Andersonville, Georgia, are the resting places of Union military men who were hanged by their fellow prisoners on July 11, 1864, for robbing the weak and helpless of food and clothing, and even murdering them. They were John Sarsfield, 144th New York; William Collins, 88th Pennsylvania; Charles Curtis, Battery A, Rhode Island Artillery; Pat Delaney, 83rd Pennsylvania; A. Munn, U.S. Navy; and W. R. Rickson, U.S. Navy. For years the graves were unmarked, but eventually they were granted the dignity of gravestones ("Six Unhallowed Graves" 2).

A few weeks before the Battle of Perryville, Kentucky, in 1862, Confederate General Braxton Bragg quartered in Nelson County. He gave his men strict orders not to forage and steal civilians' property. Those who didn't listen soon regretted it. A writer noted in 1900 that the area had gravesites of several soldiers who had found out via military tribunal that Bragg wasn't kidding. The writer noted one untended and largely forgotten grave on the Rowan farm, originally marked with a wooden slab that had since disappeared. A beech tree nearby bore the carved inscription "Thou shalt live again." The man sleeping under the myrtle was Alex Moody, a Mississippian who had forfeited his life for stealing chickens ("A Soldier's Lone Grave" 4).

A journalist saw Joseph Minix of Company A, 9th Kentucky Volunteer Infantry, get shot by a firing squad in Murfreesboro, Tennessee, explaining that "I had never witnessed an execution." Minix had been arrested on March 12, 1863, and the curious reporter was permitted to visit him in the guardhouse just before the sentence was carried out. Minix was not handcuffed nor did he wear a ball and chain, and he had only two guards, a nice display of trust in a deserter. At 8:30 a.m. on June 16, the "remarkably calm" prisoner left the guardhouse to meet his destination in an open field a mile from town, followed by a military band, the twelve-man firing squad, and pallbearers toting his casket. Minix was led to a certain spot. The squad marched twelve paces from the prisoner and turned, facing him. The band members scrambled on the double quick to get out of firing range. Minix was allowed a few minutes to pray with the chaplain. An official blindfolded him as he sat on the edge of his open coffin. Many soldiers averted their gaze; those who did missed seeing Minix's face turn pale, then blood red, then pale again, all within seconds. The Provost Marshall gave the order to fire. Afterwards, the troops were ordered to walk by the coffin and look as an object lesson. The spectacle was plenty for the writer, who noted, "Those who had never seen an execution thought one victim would satisfy them forever, among which number was your correspondent" ("Execution of Joseph Minix" 1).

A Confederate veteran reminiscing to a reporter in 1890 recounted the case of Henry K. Roberts of Tullahoma, Tennessee, whom he recalled was executed more or less "for being a fool." Roberts, a Unionist, had the misfortune to be conscripted into the Southern Army. He deserted and joined the Union army. He was recaptured in late September or early October 1863 and taken to the site where the Battle of Missionary Ridge soon would be enacted. Had Roberts kept quiet he might have been considered a prisoner of war and survived to the end of the conflict, or he might have escaped again.

Troops gathering at Petersburg, VA, to see the hanging of William Johnson of the 23rd Regiment, United States Colored Troops, on June 20, 1864. (*Library of Congress Prints and Photographs Division*)

He had grown a beard and wore a Union outfit, so it was unlikely he would have been recognized. But for some reason even he probably did not fully comprehend, Roberts impulsively pushed his luck by approaching his former Confederate lieutenant and speaking. What he said does not enter the record, but the officer immediately recognized him. Court-martial and a deserter's unmarked grave near a brick kiln soon followed. The old soldier who retold the story decades later pondered:

> When, a few weeks after, Grant's troops carried Missionary Ridge, they advanced right across the plain and trampled over the deserter's grave in their wild rush.... His grave was trodden so that it would be almost impossible to locate it long before the battle came on, so I presume he lies there yet in what must be an unknown grave. Someday some fellow, in digging a cellar or something of the kind may unearth what is left of him and have him reinterred in a national cemetery as one of the forgotten dead at the Battle of Missionary Ridge ("A Military Execution" 20.)

General Dodge's scouts captured rebel spy Samuel Davis 6 miles from Pulaski, Tennessee, at the end of November 1863. They found a pass signed by Confederate General Braxton Bragg in his pocket, as well as documents revealing the number and position of nearby Federal troops. In the face of such evidence, it seems Davis could hardly have denied being a spy, yet that's what he did at his trial, though he did plead guilty to carrying secret mail to the rebels. A fine distinction, one might think. The Union army found him guilty on both counts. A scaffold was erected hastily on a bluff northeast of town, and Davis rode to this scenic spot sitting on his coffin on November 27. As death beckoned, the officials offered Davis a deal: a full pardon if he would reveal the whereabouts of his captain. He replied scornfully. "Would you betray a friend? I had rather die a thousand deaths!" Just before mounting the stairs he chuckled to the Provost Marshal, Captain Armstrong, "I'll soon be out of your way." Three minutes later, Davis's soul was on its way to wherever it was heading. Something about seeing a man hanged must have awakened the poetic instinct in the reporter, as he ended with this effusion: "[He was] buried in the cemetery. That night evergreens were planted, and now sigh in the wild wintry winds o'er his grave, while flowers culled by fair hands, were strewn upon it" ("Execution of a Rebel Spy" 1). Davis must have made an impression on the local ladies in his brief time.

When Ephraim S. Dodd enlisted, he assured his stepmother Nannie that he would not be killed on the battlefield. He was right, but what happened was arguably not a much better fate. Acting as a Confederate spy for Company D, Terry's Texas Rangers, he was caught in Sevier County, Tennessee, in January 1864 and sentenced to be hanged in Knoxville. As he rode in a wagon down Gay Street in a light snowfall, an accompanying band played Chopin's "Death March," followed by a hardly more cheerful contemporary number entitled "Mary's Dream." Dodd's execution did not go flawlessly. The rope was made of cotton, not hemp, and it snapped after the trapdoor opened. Instead of dangling in air, Dodd lay flat on the frozen ground as "a murmur of horror, mingled with expressions of pity, ran through the assembled crowd," said an eyewitness. The prisoner, with an unbroken neck and impeccable manners, remarked, "Release me quick, if you please." But it was the officers' disagreeable duty to carry out the sentence. Rather than get a different rope like sensible beings, they doubled up the cotton noose and placed the knot behind the prisoner's head instead of behind the ear as recommended. Ten minutes later, Dodd was dead from long strangulation ("Execution of Dodd at Knoxville" 4).

A couple of weeks later, the *Louisville Journal* reprinted a lengthy, sad letter Dodd had written on January 6, two days before the hanging, to his staunch Unionist father Travis Dodd in Richmond, Kentucky. After telling the detailed story of how he was captured, Ephraim concluded, "Do not grieve for me, my dear parents, for I am leaving a world full of crime and sin for one of perfect bliss. I can say no more" ("To the editors..." 1).

On April 29, 1864, Pennsylvanian Thomas Martin Smith also became the victim of a bungled execution. Convicted of attempting to furnish the South with munitions, Smith was sentenced to be hanged at Fort Pickering in Memphis. He admitted his guilt on the scaffold and said that he deserved what he was about to receive, which turned out to be a protracted strangulation rather than a swift neck-breaking. When the horror show was over, officials speculated that the problem was that the gallows was constructed of green wood which had been soaked in a rainstorm on the night of April 27. Thus, the trapdoor was too swollen to open quickly. However, Smith received a fine compliment from an admiring observer, who noted that through his ordeal he "exhibited a becoming degree of composure, betraying not even once the least emotion favoring of fear" ("Execution at Memphis" 1).

A large part of Lincoln's reputation as a humanitarian consists of his unwillingness to execute spies and deserters. Many times he commuted their sentences for the flimsiest of reasons. But even Lincoln's famous compassion had limits. For example, Private

William Boyle of the 1st New York Mounted Rifles murdered his superior officer and was sentenced to face the firing squad. Lincoln commuted his sentence to life in prison at hard labor. However, Boyle's guard, Private Thomas Abrahams of the 139th New York, allowed him to escape. Boyle defected to the Confederates, where he immediately told all he knew about General Ben Butler's plan to rescue Union captives in Libby prison and on Virginia's Belle Isle. The mission was aborted when the rebels burned a bridge necessary for Northern troops to cross. Butler had Abrahams court-martialed for treason. He was found guilty and sentenced to be shot. This time around, the president did not interfere ("Sentenced to Be Shot" 1).

Mr. Stevens, a Federal soldier in the 20th Kentucky Volunteer Infantry, was to be shot in Louisville for desertion. The military tribunal chose the death date to be June 25, 1864. After the sentencing, Stevens grew morbidly depressed and lost both his health and his will to live. "He wandered in his thoughts as if in a stupor," said a reporter. On June 23, twenty-four hours before the sentence was to be carried out, Stevens died in prison "of remorse," said the press ("Died in Prison" 3). Mounting terror probably also played a role.

Robert Cobb Kennedy, a Confederate captain and spy from Louisiana, was also an arsonist who, along with accomplices, set fire to three New York City hotels and P. T. Barnum's museum on November 25, 1864. Today we would call him a domestic terrorist. The national press was aghast at his ill-mannered behavior on the Fort Lafayette gallows on March 25, 1865. As the death warrant was read, he kept interrupting with bitter, sarcastic laughter and the phrase "It's a damned lie." He refused to kneel in prayer with the chaplain and "seemed scarcely human in his levity," in the scandalized *New York Times*'s words. As his cap was adjusted, he favored witnesses with a song in a bogus Irish accent: "Trust to luck, trust to luck / Stare your fate in the face / Sure your heart will be aisy [*sic*] / If it's in the right place." The last word echoed spookily in the chamber as the trap door opened. The hangman, incidentally, was a deserter from Maine whose crime was pardoned since he agreed to be executioner ("Kennedy's Execution" 8; "Robert Cobb Kennedy..." 3). He did an excellent job for an amateur.

Nathaniel Marks, a member of a band of guerrillas which had terrorized Morgan County, Kentucky, was sentenced to be hanged in Louisville on January 20, 1865. The sentence was arguably pointless as he was in the final stages of tuberculosis. A reporter who saw Marks trudge to the gallows described him as pale, emaciated, and with lips covered in fever blisters. The prisoner himself remarked that the authorities were "robbing him of but a few weeks of life." Before the trap opened, he said weakly, "Amen, bless the Lord. I am going home. Sweet Jesus..." But the drop was merely three feet and Marks died of strangulation. The hanging took place at the government wood yard on the corner of East and Walnut Streets, a location generally used for circuses visiting town ("To Be Hung" 3; "Execution of Nathaniel Marks" 3).

"Guerrillas at large, take warning!" thundered the *Louisville Journal*. The occasion was the impending hanging in the city of J. J. Straney of Meade County for that crime. The execution was set for April 19, 1865. (Note the irony. He was scheduled to die slightly more than a week after the war ended.) An editorialist thought it amusing to describe, in medically accurate terminology, what Straney would soon confront: "[H]e will be suddenly suspended between the earth and the sky. This movement will either dislocate his neck or cause a contraction of his larynx. He will be left dangling until all his convulsive efforts to breathe have ceased, and until the surgeon is satisfied that he will not resuscitate until Gabriel sounds the reveille" ("Another Guerrilla to Be Hung Tomorrow" 3; "While Thinking of J. Wilkes Booth…" 3). If Straney read these words before the big event, they could not have furnished him with much comfort, which perhaps was the point. Some readers must have thought the editorial was in bad taste because the paper apologized two days later. "The editors of the *Journal* sincerely and deeply regret the very mean and silly article on the expected execution of Straney, which appeared in the local columns of the paper.… The article, which was not seen by the editors until its publication, was written by the junior reporter (a novice in the business), and we pledge our readers that their sense of propriety shall not be similarly shocked in the future" ("The editors of the *Journal*…" 2).

For the record, Straney—who was not actually hanged until April 27—met his fate with an indifference that puzzled all. Major General John M. Palmer had wanted to pardon Straney but could find zero evidence of good character, even before he became a guerrilla. Though he was hanged in an enclosure, women filled the windows of surrounding houses hoping to get a peek. When it was all over, Straney's body was sent to his mother in Bullitt County. One of the spectators remarked with the satisfied air of a prophet who lives to see his prediction come true, "When this feller was but fifteen years old I saw him kill a man, and I said he would be hung" ("Execution of J. J. Straney" 3).

Lexington, Kentucky, saw a double military execution on August 18, 1865. Guerrilla John T. Bishop, white, was to hang for killing Dr. Jeffries; the other condemned man was Aaron Collins, a black Federal soldier who had slain Matthew Currant. Both murders occurred in Bourbon County. Despite the astronomical odds against such a thing, during the execution both ropes broke. The second attempt was successful. Just as Marks had been hanged on circus grounds in Louisville, the Lexington execution occurred near a racetrack ("John T. Bishop…" 3).

One of the last Confederate military executions—if not the last—had a bitter aftertaste. In April 1865, Colonel Henry Giltner's Kentucky troops were crossing the Alleghanies hoping to join General Fitzhugh Lee. Rumors of the Confederacy's imminent collapse led men to go AWOL. The commanders felt the only cure for desertion fever was to hang the next man caught attempting it. On the night of April 10 two enlisted men from what later became Elliot County, brothers John and David May, were captured when sneaking past the picket line. Within an hour, the Mays were court-martialed and sentenced to be shot at 8 a.m. the next morning. The trial was conducted so quickly and quietly that when soldiers gathered at dawn under orders, none had any idea an execution was scheduled. Perhaps Giltner's officers thought the lesson would stick better if it came as an unpleasant surprise. The Mays were summarily shot and buried. And then came the tragic irony. The troops later found out that Lee had surrendered at Appomattox on April 9, the day before the Mays were arrested ("By Order of Court-Martial" 6).

At the outbreak of war, Dr. Thomas Clark of Rensselaer County, New York, abandoned his family and joined the army. They received word in 1861 that he had been shot for desertion, and a pine board headstone near Union Mills, Virginia, seemed to confirm it. But in spring 1874, a living, breathing Dr. Clark returned to family in Johnsonville. How had he escaped? As in *A Tale of Two Cities*, he had convinced a fellow prisoner to exchange clothes the night before his execution day and escaped.

Clark fled on board a steamer to start a new life as a surgeon, but it was hard luck on the patsy who was executed in his place, no doubt after a volley of strident protests ("A singular tragedy..." 2).

W. D. Underwood of Roanoke County, Virginia, was sentenced to be shot for desertion. His wife secured a pardon from President Jefferson Davis and then hurried to the camp as fast as she could go. As she entered camp she met the firing squad, which had just done its duty. Brooding over the tragedy drove her insane. She was committed to the Staunton Asylum in 1870 and was confined in the Salem jail in 1874 ("Mrs. C.A. Underwood..." 2).

On July 4, 1863, Confederate General John H. Winder ordered that two Union captains in Libby Prison be executed in retaliation after General Burnside hanged two rebel captains. But which two? There were seventy-five such captives to choose from. Confederate Captain T. N. Turner told the assembled captains to select among themselves at lot which two should be sacrificed. "Let Chaplain Brown do the job!" said Captain Henry Washington Sawyer of the 1st New Jersey Cavalry. The chaplain, from the 5th Maryland Regiment, reached into a box containing scraps of paper on which were written the names of each captain. He drew out a slip and handed it to Turner, who called out "Henry Washington Sawyer," leaving Sawyer and Brown looking like characters from an Ambrose Bierce war story. The other man chosen was Captain Flynn of the 51st Indiana Infantry. The two were kept pending their execution date, July 14, in a dungeon so damp their clothes mildewed. In the meanwhile, Sawyer's wife pulled strings with influential friends, who in turn urged help from President Lincoln and the secretary of war. It happened that the sons of Confederate Generals Winder and Robert E. Lee were Federal prisoners of war, and word was sent to Winder that if he executed Sawyer and Flynn, his son and Lee's would likewise die. Winder got the hint. Sawyer survived the war and died in Cape May, N.J., on October 16, 1893; Flynn's health, however, was so broken by seven weeks in the Libby dungeon that he died six months after his release (Stevens 316-24).

5

Draft Dodging

We glorify the brave soldiers on either side of the Civil War who volunteered or were drafted into service, who fought nobly, and who lived the rest of their lives (if they survived) dealing with emotional and/or physical trauma. These are stories about their opposites—men who decided that, for one reason or another, they were not about to serve in the military if they could avoid it. They appear here in ascending order of desperation: firstly, the ones who hired substitutes; secondly, the draft dodgers (a term in use even then); and thirdly, the most stubborn of all—the self-mutilators.

As is well known, for a time Northern draftees could pay a substitute to fight in their place. Even President Lincoln did so. He was exempt from the draft as the commander in chief, but he wanted to set an example, so John S. Staples of Pennsylvania fought in Lincoln's stead (Garrison *More Civil* 152).

Consider the interesting case of Frank Lander of Hawesville, Kentucky. He and his favorite slave were both drafted into the Union army in October 1864. The frightened servant did not desire to enter a soldier's uncertain existence, so Lander hired a substitute—a white man—to take his place for $900. That matter solved, there was the ticklish matter of hiring one for himself. It took several days until Lander finally found a man willing to go in his stead, but for a while it looked as though the master would enter the service and the slave would go free, of the military, at least ("Interesting Case: A Good Master" 3).

Perhaps less well known is the fact that Southern draftees also could pay substitutes. It was noted in January 1862 that so many Tennesseans wanted to hire them that the demand far exceeded the supply—which, as any economist could predict, meant that the market price rose with every passing day ("Thousands of the persons drafted..." 2). Newspapers in Richmond, Virginia, published numerous advertisements in the winter of '62 from men seeking proxies. For example, the *Dispatch* ran an ad on February 27 by Thomas B. Rees, who appears to have served as a broker—a professional seeker of replacements for the desperate. "WANTED ... Ten substitutes for a good artillery company ... I will pay a bonus of from $300 to $600 cash" ("Loud Calls for Substitutes" 4). The modern equivalent of those sums is roughly $6,220 and $12,400, so they did not come cheap.

An editorial in the *Louisville Journal* of April 25, 1862, demonstrates how quickly demand exploded: "A thousand dollars [$20,700 in modern currency] is the price now paid in the Southern Confederacy for substitutes under the conscript law. A few months ago, plenty could be had at fifty dollars [now, $1,040] per head. So the price has increased twenty fold..." ("A thousand dollars is the price..." 2). The hiring of stand-ins became such a problem that as early as April 1862, army recruiters in Baltimore offered a $1,000 sign-on bonus for men willing to fight personally ("A rebel agent..." 2.).

Then there were those who made hefty sums exploiting the substitution system. A Mr. Biesering of Weisenberg, Pennsylvania, was so alarmed when drafted in December 1862 that he hired barber William Mohr to go in his place for $1,000. Instead of enlisting, the barber found someone willing to substitute for him at a cut-rate fee of $400. Mohr made a profit of $600 by not fulfilling his military duty ("Profitable Speculation" 1).

"Let the buyer beware"—and that includes those who would pay someone to do their soldiering. A deserter from Boston, Massachusetts, was reported in September 1863 to have sold himself six times as a substitute, always running off with the money and leaving his clients in an interesting predicament. He tried it a seventh time, once too many. He was arrested and sentenced to face a firing squad ("A gay deserter..." 3).

In a case from Carroll County, Kentucky, James Cockerill paid Thomas Walsh a staggering $1,200 to be his replacement. On September 30, 1864, Walsh passed his physical exam in the Provost Marshal's office in Covington. While waiting in line to get his uniform he had second thoughts. He leaped from a second-floor window and escaped pursuers, clad only in a pair of pants and waving a fistful of greenbacks ("A Substitute Runs Away..." 4).

Closely related to hiring a substitute was the practice of eliminating the middleman by simply buying your way out of service—that is, for a brief time, men who could afford it paid the Federal government a fee, usually $300, thereby purchasing an exemption from the draft ("The War Department has definitely concluded" 3). If that sounds like legalized bribery, many people at the time thought so too, but the government considered it a quick way to fill war coffers. The policy was carried out informally for a while, but the War Department made it binding in July 1863, when Provost Marshal General James B. Fry announced that commissioners of Internal Revenue (forerunners of the IRS) would collect the money and provide a receipt, no doubt gorgeously engraved in the style of the time, declaring that the bearer was officially exempt and unofficially $300 poorer ("The Three Hundred Dollars Exemption" 1).

The exchange of cash for immunity led to this shameless ad which appeared in a Geneva, New York, newspaper in April 1863: "Wanted: Four industrious young men wish to marry four respectable young ladies who enjoy a fortune of $300 each, to evade the draft" ("Matrimony has proved a good speculation..." 1). They might as well have come straight to the point and said, "Buy our way out of military service and we will marry you."

The policy of allowing the well-heeled—or those who could scrape up $300 somehow—to escape the draft was short-lived. A Congressional bill to repeal the exemption clause was introduced by Senator Wilson (the author of the original bill!) on December 8, 1863, a scant five months after it had passed ("The notice of the bill..." 1). A report dated December 24 noted, "[The Senate] will strike out the exemption clause.... The feeling is general that the Army must be filled up and the war vigorously prosecuted to an end" ("The sentiment of the Senate respecting..." 1). Evidently, even though the fee was a hefty $300, a price that would seem unsurmountable for most men at the time, too many were exploiting the loophole to get off the hook.

American men who wished to avoid service in Vietnam were notorious for fleeing to Canada. One wonders how many knew that some of their ancestors during the

Civil War—from both sides of the conflict—did the very same thing. For example, the *Cincinnati Commercial* of August 6, 1862, complained about the number of young unmarried men who had left for Canada in the last few days ("Shameful" 1).

The *Toronto Leader* remarked in November 1861 that huge numbers of Americans had fled to Quebec and Montreal, "but even here it is considerable, and with a certainty of increase" ("Refugees from Northern Despotism" 4). Many were former British immigrants to the USA who decided maybe they should go to Canada and re-declare allegiance to the queen after all. Windsor—just opposite the border from Detroit—was reportedly teeming with nervous Yanks and Rebs in March 1863 ("At Windsor, Canada..." 1). There were so many in St. Catherines by April that, reportedly, "the authorities are beginning to fear for the propriety, morals, and welfare of the genuine citizens," which implies that many of the "absquatulators" weren't citizens of the highest quality ("The *St. Catharines*" 2). In April 1864, it was estimated that an astonishing 15,000 deserters and draft dodgers were hiding in Canada and competing with the native-born for jobs ("It is believed..." 4). Some resentful young Canadians immigrated to the USA to seek employment ("Working Both Ways" 1).

On August 9, 1862, Secretary of War Stanton announced that men caught sneaking off to Canada would be severely punished. As a sort of consolation prize, captured fleers would at least be given the opportunity to choose which regiment to join ("Draft Dodgers in Difficulty" 3). The *Cleveland Herald* warned would-be skedaddlers that it would be almost impossible to get past the city and that their wisest course was to stay home and volunteer ("Draft Dodgers in Difficulty" 3).

At last, Canadians got so fed up with encroachers from America that on September 21, 1864, the government threatened to draft escapees from both armies into the British Army. As the Crown put it, "Refugees or exiles seeking protection of this government must lend their aid to strengthen the government that gives them protection" ("Those who have escaped..." 1). Some Americans sheepishly crossed the border back into their native country to take their chances; others shrugged and joined the British, figuring that, well, at least England isn't at war with anyone right now.

Some draft dodgers had subtler methods than fleeing north. Men who didn't see the glory in having their heads taken off by flying cannonballs possessed endless wellsprings of creativity. It was reported in August 1862 that a drafted drayman knocked the heel off one of his boots and entered the doctor's office with a pronounced, though artificial, limp. Fortunately for him, the physician did not look closely and signed a certificate of exemption due to "defective limbs," after which the drayman presumably returned to his regular job of delivering beer to taverns ("A Drafting Dodge" 1).

A New Jersey millionaire was caught taking a steamer to Europe in August 1862. He had disguised himself as a stoker, workers who shoveled coal into the ship's engine furnaces ("A New Jersey millionaire..." 2).

A perfectly healthy black hotel waiter in Hartford, Connecticut, got his draft notice *circa* August 1863 and hatched a scheme. He sent another man with a lame knee to impersonate him at the doctor's office. The plan was sound, except in a couple of particulars. First, the impostor's knee wasn't lame enough to earn an exemption, and the doctor declared him fit for service. Second, he did not wish to join the army, and he confessed. In the end, the waiter entered the ranks anyway and his stooge likely went to jail for attempting to defraud the government ("At Hartford" 1).

A Cleveland, Ohio, man applied for an exemption in August 1863 on the grounds that he had to take care of his poor, feeble old mother. The depth of the fellow's filial affection may be estimated by the fact that he had a coffin for his mother right there in the cellar, just awaiting the moment when it would fulfill its purpose. In the meanwhile, he stored turnips in it ("An Affectionate Son" 1).

When dodgers discovered that married men could be exempt from the draft—though not always—that was all it took for lifelong bachelors to decide that maybe this thing called love was worth checking out after all. A *Louisville Journal* editorial remarked on April 25, 1863, "The passage of the Conscription Act is driving all the young men into the bonds of love and matrimony.... It will more than double the brides and the population" ("Conscription vs. Matrimony" 1). The paper remarked in the same issue, "We are sorry, however, that the young women are willing to become the wives and the probable mothers of cowards" ("Men are marrying at the East..." 1).

As with substitutes, unscrupulous souls made money by exploiting dodgers' fears. A man in Michigan published advertisements stating that he could provide a foolproof way to escape the draft—for the low, low price of one dollar. Tremulous men who sent a buck got a one-word reply by return mail: Enlist. "His advice, if followed, was worth ten times what he charged for it," remarked one newspaper ("The Michigan gentleman..." 2).

Some draftees took out their contempt on enrollment officers. One, Fletcher Freeman, was murdered while traveling in Sullivan County, Indiana, in June 1863 ("Cincinnati: In Boone County..." 1). In August 1863 at Jarrettsville, Maryland, arsonists burned the barns of two such officers and someone fired six shots into the house of enroller Levi Pennington ("Some indications of resistance to the draft..." 1).

On the other hand, some of the strongest resistance to the draft came not from men but from the women they would be leaving. In November 1862 the Draft Commissioner of Ozaukee County, Wisconsin, had his new conscripts all rounded up. They seemed resigned to their fate and willing to go, but their wives and girlfriends—described as "Amazons"—had other ideas, and they pounced on the government official with clubs, bludgeons, stones, and probably not a few other down-homey weapons. They broke both the commissioner's head and the draft box, and he had to telegraph to Milwaukee for help. A news dispatch dated November 15 hastily explained that this attitude was not common among Badger Staters: "In justice to the loyal people of Wisconsin, it is proper to state that the recent draft troubles [were] principally confined to a class of Germans called Luxembergers. Over one hundred have been arrested in Ozaukee County, and the draft is being enforced promptly" ("The Women the Cause of the Resistance..." 1; "Milwaukee: In justice..." 3).

On June 15, 1863, women pelted an enrolling officer with eggs as men held him down in Boone County, Indiana ("Cincinnati: In Boone County..." 1). A few days later in Terre Haute, a woman threw boiling oil and water on enrollment officer B. M. Harrison, scalding him badly. Then she brained the marshal who came to arrest her with a hot poker ("At Terre Haute..." 1).

One of the surest ways to get out of the service—for a while, anyway, until the authorities got wise—was to maim yourself. One cannot handle a gun very well if missing one or more fingers, thus some men who did not wish to be mutilated on the battlefield chose a more voluntary, though no less permanent, form of mutilation by declaring open war on their own digits. It was reported in August 1862 that four men in

Danbury, Connecticut, demanded a certificate of exemption from the draft board. Three had cut off the trigger fingers of their right hands, and the fourth severed that finger on his left hand—having somehow mistaken his left hand for his right ("Cowardly Self-Mutilation" 3).

On October 6, 1862, G. W. Ewing was drafted in LaPorte County, Indiana. On October 15, he did something about it by shooting the fingers off his right hand. The army countered that they would take him anyway, but one wonders in what conceivable capacity ("Maimed Himself" 3).

In August 1863, an Ohio man reportedly avoided serving Uncle Sam by amputating his hand via passing locomotive ("It is reported in an Ohio paper..." 1). In the same month, a Washington, D.C., man slashed his throat to avoid the draft. But he was a novice at this fine art. He survived and was forced into the military by unsympathetic officials ("A Negro in Washington..." 1).

John Trulock of Jeffersonville, Indiana, was drafted in November 1864. After he passed his physical, he chopped two fingers off his left hand. "John is a fool," sneered the *Louisville Journal*. "Two fingers won't let him out" ("A Fool: John Trulock..." 3). The comment suggests that by that point in the war, missing digits were no longer a dealbreaker.

A Civil War soldier had to have a good set of teeth, since he often had to tear open paper cartridges with his incisors. As soon as this became general knowledge, many young men asked themselves, "Front teeth? Who needs 'em, anyway?" One draftee in Portland, Kentucky, had four extracted in July 1863 ("An 'Exemption' Trick" 1). A man in Amesbury, Massachusetts, had eight removed in May 1864. When the government found out the facts, the Amesbury man was arrested and forced to serve in the artillery after all ("A man at Amesbury, Mass..." 3). So many attempted this stunt that the War Department declared in September 1862 that toothlessness would no longer be considered a reason to escape the draft, but clearly this did not stop men from trying it ("Persons without front teeth..." 2).

Sometimes the mutilations were not voluntary. In June 1861, the *Cincinnati Press* told of a soldier from the 2nd Ohio Brigade who had been granted a few days' furlough at home. He returned to Camp Dennison with his finger wrapped in a rag. He explained that his wife had so objected to his enlisting for three years that she cut off one of his fingertips with a chisel and mallet while he was asleep. But it was all, all for nothing. He was a drummer, so missing a fingertip did not affect his service. He insisted on going, and he went ("A volunteer in the Second Brigade..." 4).

A similar fate befell Samuel Dickinson of Sanilac Township, Michigan. On November 1, 1861, Captain Huckins gave an enlistment speech before an enthusiastic crowd at Maskell's schoolhouse. Mr. Dickinson, afflicted with war fever, signed the muster roll. This displeased Mrs. Dickinson, who felt actions speak louder than words. The next night, she waited until he was asleep and placed his hand on the bed railing. Then she positioned the dull blade of a shaving razor on two fingers on his right hand and hit the razor with a billet of wood. Off came the fingers with a neatness and professionalism that would have done credit to a battlefield surgeon. On the plus side, she made sure she had cloth handy to make a tourniquet and bind the wound. Dickinson must have appreciated her wifely concern, for afterward he said he "had brought it upon himself" and could not blame her ("All for Love" 1).

6

The Ironies of War

Veteran Ambrose Bierce became, in later life, a journalist, acid-tongued satirist, and author of strange and grotesque fiction. He fought in an inconclusive skirmish near Greenbrier River in Pocahontas County, Virginia (now West Virginia), on October 3, 1861. Only eight of Bierce's fellow Union soldiers were killed, but he recalled one who went out in an oddly appropriate fashion. J. A. Abbott was struck by a cannonball on which was imprinted the name of the foundry that manufactured it: Abbott (Morris 30).

"Hey, you've been drafted!" So the friends of a young man in Providence, Rhode Island, informed him in summer 1863. Men who were drafted against their will didn't get anything for joining, but volunteers could reap a signing-on bonus. The young man hurried to the recruiting office to get a bounty for enlisting, hoping that he could sign the paperwork before word of his drafting got to the officials.

After the forms were signed and the young man was obligated to face deprivation, hardships, and possible death in a thousand grisly forms, he ascertained that his witty pals had played a practical joke on him. He had not been drafted at all ("In Providence last week..." 3).

Impoverished civilian refugees Mr. and Mrs. Morton Eastman journeyed on foot to Wheeling, West Virginia, in early November 1864. Along the way, Mrs. Eastman died of exposure and fatigue. The widower bought the best coffin he could afford and arranged to have the body shipped by freight to Alton, Illinois, where he intended to relocate. When Eastman and coffin arrived at their destination, he removed the lid and beheld not his late wife but a very young soldier. Meanwhile, the soldier's mourners opened what they took to be his casket and found Mrs. Eastman instead. The railroad estimated that the two coffins got switched somewhere between Columbus and Cincinnati, and all was made right ("A Strange Story, If True" 3).

Colonel Frederick Benteen's men were pursuing Confederate Major-General Sterling Price through the wilds of Missouri in December 1864. One cold night as they camped at Carthage, they set a fire to what they took to be a log. As the flames crackled away with false cheer, they realized that the "log" was really a dead rebel. They extinguished the fire and gave him a Christian burial, but a nearby family was so spooked that they packed up and moved immediately ("Dead Rebel Taken for a Back-Log" 3).

Soldier Harvey Maxwell wanted out of the army so badly that he fatally slit his throat at Camp Carrington, near Gallipolis, Ohio, in mid-March 1865. A few hours later, his friends showed up with a substitute in tow whom they had hired to take his place ("The Suicide at Camp Carrington" 1).

First day on the job: on June 27, 1862, Confederate Colonel Isaac Gurdon Seymour was at last appointed to lead the 6th Louisiana Infantry Regiment in the charge at the Battle at Gaines' Mill, Virginia (aka the Battle of Chickahominy River). He survived his promotion by only a few hours (Garrison *Civil War Curiosities* 200).

Southern civilians gained a reputation for hiding money and family heirlooms in areas soon to be occupied by Northern soldiers, and the Union men gained their own reputation for looking for the loot when time allowed. It was reported in May 1865 that General Sherman's men were such avid treasure-seekers during the March to the Sea that different squads exhumed and reburied the same dead mule six times. Someone finally left its head sticking out above the surface so it could slumber in peace ("Gen. Sherman's 'bummers'..." 3).

As leader of the 85th Pennsylvania Infantry, Union Colonel Joshua B. Howell made his way through the Battles of Yorktown, Williamsburg, Seven Pines, the Seven Days, Fort Wagner, and the Bermuda Hundred with minor wounds, all between April 1862 and May 1864. He fell off his horse on September 12, 1864, and died two days later (Garrison *Civil War Curiosities* 201).

The last slave sold in the South went on sale in Richmond, Virginia, near the end the war. The asking price was 900 cabbages. In those final famished days of the Confederacy, a cabbage went for a dollar per head (almost $14.00 in modern currency), so the slave was worth roughly nine hundred dollars ("The last slave sold in the Confederacy..." 2).

A year after the war, a Louisiana journalist recalled a heartrending scene he witnessed at the siege of Port Hudson in 1863. Two soldiers lay at a carpenter's shop with cloths covering their faces as that craftsman constructed an extra-wide coffin. Nearby sat a weeping older soldier with his arm in a sling. The mourner explained, "They were my sons and were twins. One of them joined at the same time I did. We came here with General Beale..."

That morning, one twin had been shot through the head by a Northern sharpshooter and the other was killed seconds later as he ran to his brother's aid. "As they came into the world, so they went out of it—together," said their father. "In removing their bodies from the breastworks, I got this wound which has shattered my arm." He lamented further that he was alone in the world, the twins' mother having died giving birth to them.

A few days later, as the twins' father sat in front of his tent, an exploding shell killed him too ("The Twin Brothers" 4).

Libby Prison in Richmond, Virginia—where so many men starved—was used as a grocery by January 1866 ("Libby prison..." 1).

There were many war surplus ambulances in postbellum North Carolina. So many, in fact, that in November 1866 it was reported that they had become citizens' primary mode of transportation ("The people of North Carolina..." 1).

Confederate General Benjamin Franklin Cheatham was sitting in his Nashville home on September 4, 1886, when he heard a wagon rumbling by on the street. "There go the troops," he said to his wife. "Bring me my horse. I am going to the front." After saying these words, he passed away ("Gone to the Front" 5).

Trone Wilson was born a slave in Georgia. He was in prison for being an accessory to a murder in Liberty County at the time of emancipation. The governor gave him a Christmastime pardon in 1895. He was believed to be the last slave to receive the benefits of the Emancipation Proclamation, having never been a free man in his life until his parole ("Never Was Free Before" 5).

Manassas, Virginia, devastated during the war, found that its notoriety made it a tourist attraction. As early as August 1868, its former travails had made it prosperous ("Manassas..." 2).

An epitaph reported in 1870 to be in Greenwood Cemetery in Columbia, Tennessee, on the tombstone of a former Confederate soldier who survived the war only to be killed in a street fight: "He escaped the bullets of the enemy to be assassinated by a cowardly pup" ("The following inscription..." 2).

In an 1885 interview with the *Cincinnati Enquirer*, Union General M. T. McMahon described a conversation he had with a fellow general, John Sedgwick, at the Battle of Spotsylvania Court House, Virginia, on May 9, 1864. McMahon was worried about Confederate sharpshooters: "Why, General, we have lost several officers this morning. These are telescopic rifles, and they are evidently picking out the officers." Sedgwick responded, "Oh, pshaw! I don't believe they could hit an elephant at that distance." That was the last thing Sedgwick ever said, but he died smiling ("Sedgwick's Death" 11).

7

Black Slaveowners

Long before settlers from the New World arrived, Native Americans enslaved other tribes. (And, as we shall see, their slaves weren't always other Indians.) Northwestern tribes who owned slaves included the Chinook, the Tlingit, the Tsimshian, the Nootka, the Makah, the Quileute and the Kwakiutl. Indian slaves led horrible existences because their lives were considered practically valueless. Often they were killed so they could continue serving their masters in the afterworld. Some wealthy tribesmen sacrificed them during celebrations called potlatches.

In one notorious case during the Puget Sound War of 1855–56, Chief Patkanim of the Snoqualmie and Snohomish tribes learned that the U.S. military offered a bounty of $20 for the head of each Klickitat Indian. Patkanim made a fortune selling the heads of his slaves (McQueen 133).

The famous northwestern Chief Seattle owned eight Indian slaves whom he freed only after the signing of the Emancipation Proclamation (McCarthy).

The national press mentioned the death of "Old Chip," a Chippewa. The Winnebago tribe near the Canadian border captured him in his youth. Different tribes enslaved him over the years. After 1830 he was owned by a tribe near South Bend, Indiana, where he died on March 5, 1891, allegedly at age 105 ("In Abolitionist Indiana" 5).

Meanwhile, in the southeast, the Cherokee enslaved members of other tribes, then gradually blacks as well, many of whom worked on Cherokee-owned plantations in northern Georgia. By 1825 Indians in that region owned as many as 1,227 black slaves. Many of these slaveholding Cherokee were of mixed blood, but some were full blooded (Starkey 18-19, 320). In 1850, the Cherokee announced a plan to tax all free blacks living within their territory ("The Council of the Cherokees" 3). Many who decry the Trail of Tears—the forced removal of southern Indians from their land by President Jackson—seem unaware of an outrage within the outrage: many of these displaced Indians owned black slaves and brought them on the journey.

Other southeastern tribes known to have owned black slaves include the Creek, the Chickasaw, the Choctaw, and the Seminole (Wilson 491). The Creek Nation owned so many that it was estimated in 1901 that out of 16,000 members, 6,000 were black. "So influential ... are the former slaves of the Creek Nation that one of the most prominent of its head chiefs was L. C. Perryman, a man of Negro descent and appearance"

("Negroes in the Creek Nation" 3). By December 1850, the combined Cherokee, Choctaw, Chickasaw, Creek, and Seminole tribes owned so many slaves—while being pushed off their land by white settlers—the *Fort Smith Herald* predicted that they would form their own slave state ("A Slave State in Embryo" 2).

In the words of Catholic historian Gary Potter, "Received knowledge ... will be further thrown into confusion if it is mentioned that among the Confederacy's Native American allies were planters with slaveholdings greater than were possessed by all but a handful of the small minority of white Southerners who owned slaves." The deeper we dig, the less tidy history looks.

Amazingly, some tribes owned slaves long after 1865. This will surprise those who think only whites owned slaves and that the Civil War put a definitive end to slavery. For example, on May 5, 1883, D. M. Riordan, an official in the Navajo Indian agency, wrote to the commissioner of Indian Affairs from Fort Defiance, Arizona, about a distressing situation. Despite the Emancipation Proclamation, an estimated 300 Indians were still being held as slaves by the Navajo, "some of whom are war captives, while others are the results of trades or purchases. The descendants of these ... are always considered slaves." Riordan wrote further: "The owners of slaves have always held that they have absolute power over them and thought as little of killing one of them as they would a dog. They beat and starved them as the mood possessed, and, in short, acted toward them as slave drivers generally do." The matter came to Riordan's attention after one Navajo killed his slave, a little Moqui boy whose entire family had been slaves for four generations. The slave's father rashly had declared that his son had a right to be free, and the boy was murdered to teach the father a lesson. Riordan's account ended with the promising news that the Navajo had agreed to free their slaves ("Slavery Not Extinct" 5).

Ten long years after the end of the Civil War, the Chickasaw and Choctaw were still denying rights to their former slaves. The following news article from September 1875, datelined Muskogee, proves additionally that while we hear much about whites violating treaties, Native Americans would break agreements with the U.S. government if they found it advantageous:

> J. P. C. Shanks, special United States Commissioner, arrived in the Territory to-day. He is on his way to the Chickasaw Nation, to attend their National Council, now in session at Tishimingo, with a view to settle the future status of the colored people held as slaves by the Indians before emancipation. By a provision of the treaty of 1866, the United States agreed to pay to the Choctaws and Chickasaws the proceeds of the sale of leased lands west of ninety-eight degrees, owned by them, the sum of three hundred thousand dollars, contingent upon their admitting their former slaves and their descendants to the rights of citizenship and forty acres of land in the nation, or failing to do this, the United States were to remove the colored people at the end of thirty days from the expiration of two years, deducting that amount from their national funds and apply[ing] it to the expense of their removal from the limits of the nation, which has not been done. It is to be hoped the vexed question will be definitely settled now, as much dissatisfaction has grown out of the non-fulfillment of the treaty. ("Negroes Among the Indians" 1)

Members of Florida's swamp-dwelling Seminole tribe still owned black slaves in 1890, twenty-five years after the end of the war that allegedly freed them. The Seminole reasoned that since they were not considered American citizens, they were not bound to obey laws passed by American legislators. When President Chester Arthur beseeched the tribe to free its slaves, Chief Tallahassee advised him to go to hell ("Slavery in Florida" 6).

Little is said about Native owners of slaves, and even less about other American ethnic groups who also possessed humans. Consider Anthony Johnson of Northampton County, Virginia, one of the first slaveholders in America and sometimes referred to as the "Father of Slavery in the United States."

When black laborers were first introduced to this country, they were not always held for lifelong servitude—another fact known to few modern Americans. Black workers were usually held for only a certain number of years (generally seven) and then set free, as were (mostly white) indentured servants. In colonial times, enforced servitude for life was mainly a punishment for crime for both blacks and whites, although during this period, Indians were sometimes enslaved for purely economic reasons. Historian Edgar McManus wrote, "For most of the seventeenth century Negro slaves had an equivocal legal status somewhere between indentured servitude and absolute bondage. Frequently they were referred to as servants rather than as slaves, and in some cases freedom was granted after a limited period of service" (56). Another historian, Alf Mapp, Jr., stated, "Brought to the colony as an indentured servant in 1619, [the Negro] had by the latter part of the seventeenth century become a slave" (209). Matthew Page Andrews, who specialized in Virginia history, wrote: "In view of the fact that records have been found of the release from service of some ... early Negro immigrants in Virginia, it seems reasonable to assume that all were indentured, as in the case of White servants. In 1623 in the Bermudas, also in 1625 in Virginia, questions involving Negroes came up before the courts. In both cases it is significant to note that the discussion was not concerned with the ownership of these persons but of their services" (89).

Therefore, the first black servants in America were seldom considered slaves for life. But Anthony Johnson, a dissatisfied rich landowner, changed that. He wanted to hold his servants for longer than seven years, so in 1653 he successfully petitioned the court to make servitude binding for life (WPA 76, 378). Historian Mapp flatly calls Johnson "the first Virginia planter to make a slave of his indentured servant" (209). Other states soon followed influential Virginia's lead.

And Anthony Johnson was black.

Yes, the man arguably most responsible for making slavery a lasting institution in America was himself black, wealthy, and an owner of black slaves. He is nearly forgotten today, and it isn't hard to see why. Johnson stands as a most uncomfortable reminder that history, like life, is not always (pardon the pun) black and white.

Johnson was one of the first African captives brought to America. He arrived in Virginia as an indentured servant, probably in 1619 (Bruce 564), and was himself free by about 1625 (Mapp 90). He was the first free black man and the first black landowner in Virginia, possibly in America. He founded the first black community in the New World, on Virginia's Pungoteague Creek (WPA 76, 378). As Johnson rose to financial prominence, he gained 250 acres of land and five indentured servants who gradually became his slaves. The landmark 1653 case mentioned above involved one of Johnson's runaway indentured servants, a man named John Casor, who sued Johnson in court ("with the help of white friends," let it be noted) on the grounds that Casor—to borrow the haphazard spelling of the era—"came unto Virginia for seaven or eight years of Indenture," but Johnson "had kept him his ser't seaven years longer than hee should or ought" (Andrews 89-90). Johnson asked the Northampton County court for the return of his runaway laborer and to make Casor's servitude binding for life. The court agreed, thereby establishing a legal precedent in favor of slavery: "As far as is known, this was the first judicial sanction in the English colonies of life servitude where crime was not involved" (WPA 76). Put another way, Johnson became "the first person in the colony, white or black, to hold as a lifetime servant a Negro who had committed no crime" (WPA 76).

Perhaps Anthony Johnson was merely a historical fluke? Not quite. There were many black slaveowners in America, and not only in the South. One historian writes: "The Negroes brought with them from their native land African ideas and customs. They were used from immemorial times to slavery. Many of those brought thence to America had been slaves in their own land. Others had been owners of slaves in Africa. In both cases they were used to slavery. It did not therefore seem to them unnatural for a Negro in America to hold his brethren in bondage when he had become free and able to buy his fellows" (Wilson 484).

One early record, the 1790 census, shows that in Maryland alone forty-eight free blacks owned a minimum of 143 slaves (Wilson 490). Loren Schweninger writes in the February 1990 issue of the *American Historical Review*: "By 1830, approximately 1,556 free black masters in the Deep South owned a total of 7,188 slaves. Representing about 42 percent of the black owners in the South, they owned 60 percent of the black-owned slaves." In rural Louisiana, roughly 25 percent of all free blacks owned slaves (36). Black slaveholders also lived in Florida, Kentucky, Mississippi, Missouri, Tennessee, North Carolina, Georgia, Alabama, the District of Columbia, and even Northern states such as Delaware, Massachusetts, New York, and Connecticut (Koger 1; Wilson 491, *passim*).

In 1912, slightly less than fifty years after the Civil War, Calvin Wilson could write in *Popular Science* that the story of black slaveholders had "become for our generation practically a lost chapter":

> The fact has been almost forgotten. The full data have never been collected, and probably never will be in an exhaustive way. Much material on this subject has perished through the burning of court houses, state houses, and similar depositories of documents. The generations that were familiar with this condition have gone. More than forty daily newspapers passed around from one to another during the summer of 1907 a few crumbs of information on this matter as items of curious news. Editorial comment was tinctured with surprise and in some cases with incredulity.... The bulk of the facts is still buried in unpublished documents in court houses, historical societies, and libraries. There are probably a few hundreds of people still living who have recollections of this phase of slavery. (483, 494).

Here are some specific real-life examples:

* One of the earliest deeds in the record books of St. Augustine, Florida, concerns a black carpenter named Joseph Sanchez, who sold a slave to Francisco Sanchez for $300 (Wilson 484).

* In 1797, Mobile, Alabama, was home to several black slaveholders including Juan Batista Lusser, Julia Vilard, Simon Andry, and the Forbes family (Wilson 484).
* In Mecklenburg, Virginia, *circa* 1840, a family of free blacks named Epps owned several slaves (Wilson 485).
* John Carruthers Stanly (sometimes spelled Stanley), born in 1772 in Craven County, N.C., was a mulatto owner of sixty-four slaves. At the same time, he had forty-two other blacks "bound to him by law for service" (Wilson 486). According to Schweninger, "despite his own slave heritage" Stanly was "a regular bidder at local auctions.... By the late 1820s, Stanly had become one of the leading slaveholders and wealthiest property owners in his section of North Carolina. His total estate exceeded $68,000." In addition, "One New Bern resident later recalled that Stanly was a 'hard task-master' who demanded long hours in the field and 'fed and clothed indifferently'" (42). Stanly owned two large cotton and turpentine plantations near New Bern called Lion Pasture and Hope. Some of his children also owned slaves right up to the time of the Civil War and "held them rigidly to account" (Wilson 486)—in other words, they were worked harshly.
* Nat Butler of Aberdeen, Maryland, bought and sold slaves. He was in effect a slave trader, and an underhanded one. He would persuade slaves to run away and hide on his property. Those who did were resold to other traders. "His conduct became so notorious that he lost the confidence of slave owners and respect of Negroes, who several times tried to murder him" (Wilson 487).
* Schweninger remarks that some black slavers "seemed as callous as the most profit-minded whites." For example, "South Carolina planters John and William Holman, African-born mulatto sons of English slave trader John Holman, established a 'factory' on the Rio Pong River, north of Sierra Leone, and for nearly a quarter-century, reaped huge profits buying and selling fellow Africans" (37).
* A black man in Mobile, Alabama, named Dubocra owned several slaves in his lifetime. He died in 1906, wishing to the very end that he still had them (Wilson 488-89).
* The owner of a slave blacksmith named Tom in Vance County, N.C., permitted him to hire himself out for wages. Tom gradually earned enough to purchase his own freedom around 1820 at a generously low price set by his master. Tom prospered and bought two or three slaves of his own (Wilson 491).
* Free mulattos Ciprien Ricaud (or Ricard) and his wife were extremely wealthy residents of Iberville Parish, Louisiana. They owned two plantations with an estimated combined size of 4,000 acres and at least 168 slaves, and possibly as many as 250, circa 1859 (Koger 1; Wilson 492-93), far more than most white slaveholders ever owned. The Ricauds were said to be among the richest people of any race in the South.
* Another free Louisiana black, Auguste Donatto of St. Landry Parish, owned a 500-acre cotton plantation and seventy slaves (Koger 1).
* Before the Civil War, Josephine Decuir and her husband, also of St. Landry Parish, owned 112 slaves and were worth approximately $160,000 (Schweninger 47).
* Frederick Law Olmsted wrote in 1856 of an unnamed black slaveholder in Louisiana: "The best house and most tasteful grounds that [Olmsted's informant] had visited in the State belong to a nearly full-blooded Negro—a very dark man. He and his family

are well educated, and though French is their habitual tongue, they speak English with freedom.... [T]hey owned, he presumed, a hundred slaves" (641-42).

* The largest slaveowner of color in South Carolina history was a mulatto named James Pendarvis, who owned 123 slaves according to the 1790 census. By the time of his death in 1798, he owned 155 (Koger 109).
* A large family of Louisiana blacks, the Metoyers, collectively owned nearly 400 slaves (Rollins "Black Southerners in Gray" 8).
* The Louisiana Legislature passed a bill in March 1858 preventing free blacks from holding slaves. "The practice must be quite common to require an act of the legislature to prevent it," remarked the *Louisville Courier* ("Holding Slaves" 1). The law must have had no teeth, because three months later the 1,643-acre sugar plantation of Samuel S. Harrison, deceased, near Bayou Goula, was sold for $240,500 at public auction to "a free man of color who owned the adjoining plantation." The purchaser also got ninety-five slaves ("A splendid sugar plantation" 1).
* The 1863 Emancipation Board Report reveals three slaveowning blacks who lived in Washington, D.C.: Robert Gunnell, who owned ten; Gabriel Coakley, owner of eight; James W. McDaniel, owner of two. In other words, during the height of the Civil War and after the signing of the Emancipation Proclamation, there were black slaveholders dwelling in Washington, the bastion of American liberty. D.C. held 3,100 slaves in total ("Emancipation Board" 74).
* "Aunt Eliza" of Louisville was owned by John Hunley, white, who freed her in 1833. When Hunley died a few years later, Eliza inherited a 40-acre farm and a two-story log cabin on Newburg Road, near an area Louisvillians called the Wet Woods. Eliza was described in an 1891 article: "Her chief ambition from the moment of her freedom, it seemed, was to become a slave owner and a lady." And purchase slaves Eliza did, primarily children, until at her peak she owned forty-five. A statute in effect at the time—in Louisville, at least—forbade blacks to own slaves. Eliza got around the law by transferring ownership of her slaves in trust to James Guthrie, financier. The article about this creative slaveholder notes, "While never cruel, it seems Aunt Eliza never allowed her slaves to stop work except to sleep or eat." She owned several carriages, traveled with a footman, and refused to do any work whatsoever, declaring that she "owned enough men and women to work for her." Eliza was married three times—once to a slave, but since she did not happen to possess him, he fled for Canada at the first opportunity. "She never owned any of her husbands," the account dryly noted. Eliza owned slaves until emancipation forced her to free them. When she died in 1887, she willed her cabin and farm to a woman whom she had once bought for $600—a woman described in the deed of trust as "the most valuable piece of property she had ever owned" ("A Negro Slaveholder" 2).
* John Chavis, a black man, served in the Continental Army during the Revolutionary War and attended Washington Academy (now known as Princeton). He was an educator who ran schools in four North Carolina counties. Despite being a Presbyterian minister at a time when Presbyterians were largely antislavery, he owned slaves. Chavis outspokenly referred to abolitionists as "abominable wretches" (Aurandt 62-3).
* Sally Seymour was a South Carolina slave whose owner, Thomas Martin, emancipated her in 1795. She went into business as a pastry cook in her own Charleston shop. One

might expect Seymour, who had been a slave herself, to be unwilling to use slave labor. Instead, she owned two by 1802, and eventually bought at least two others. Before her death in 1824, Seymour sold two to her daughter (Koger 38-9).

* In March 1861, a *New York Times* correspondent described another black Seymour in Charleston—William H. Seymour, age sixty-five—a gourmet chef and hotelkeeper once worth $50,000 and the owner of slaves. He had headed a regiment of black soldiers in the War of 1812 and remarked, ominously, that he was ready to take up arms again "if the damned Yankees come down here to interfere with our institutions," an event that was only about a month away ("A Wealthy Colored Individual" 4).
* Two free blacks, Margaret Mitchell Harris and her half-brother Robert Michael Collins, owned the 981-acre Santee rice plantation in the Georgetown District of South Carolina *circa* 1849. Their harvest was cultivated by a force of at least twenty-two slaves and possibly as many as thirty-seven (Koger 1, 28, 121-22).
* In 1860, the state of South Carolina held 171 free blacks who owned 766 slaves. One of the most prosperous, a mulatto cotton planter named William Ellison, owned sixty-three slaves in Charleston (Koger 18, 144-45; 190). Another was Anthony Weston, a former slave trained as a millwright, whose master emancipated him in 1826. He gradually became the owner of twenty slaves through his wife and one of the wealthiest black men in the state. In 1860 his estate was estimated to be worth nearly $50,000 (Koger 43-4). The 1860 taxpayers list shows that the city of Charleston was home to 132 persons of color who paid taxes on 390 slaves (Wilson 490). As of January 1863, the city held ninety-one free blacks who owned 268 slaves between them. Near the end of the war, there were still seventy-five black masters in the city who collectively possessed 241 slaves (Koger 18).
* Charleston had a long history of blacks and mulattos owning slaves. In 1800, nearly one out of three black heads of households in the city owned slaves. Studies by historian Larry Koger reveal that city-dwelling blacks who owned slaves tended to be women, while out in the country black slaveowners tended to be male (Koger 23-8). A 1907 article in the *Charleston News and Courier* offers a long list of non-white slaveholders who lived in that city and the number of slaves each owned: R. E. Dereef, an Indian (fourteen slaves); Maria Weston (fourteen); Amos Baxter (thirteen); Elizabeth Duprat (twelve); George Shrewsbery (twelve); R. Holloway (twelve); Phoebe Lewis (eleven); James Johnston (ten); Samuel Weston, a trustee (eight); Joseph Dereef, Indian (six); John L. Francis (seven); Peter B. Matthews (seven); Jacob Weston (seven); J.A. Sasportas (five); Louias Decoster (five); Robert Howard (five); Francis St. Marks (three); Thomas R. Small (three).

The article continued:

> [Free black slaveholders] had no political privileges [that is, they could not vote], but they were amply protected in all their civil rights and were free to buy and sell and to engage in whatever legitimate commercial enterprise or industrial undertaking they pleased. How they owned, whether by gift or by purchase, we do not know, although we were informed yesterday that these colored people bought their slaves just as slaves were purchased by the white people, and that they managed them very much in the same way. ("Many Negroes Owned Slaves" 9)

* Three days after the Civil War began the *Louisville Courier* mentioned an unnamed black woman in Charleston who owned $40,000 in real estate and owned fourteen slaves ("There is a colored woman" 1).
* A Virginia ex-slave named Gilbert Hunt owned two slaves as well as a house and $500 worth of property at the time of his death in 1863 (Jordan 65).
* A free black woman, Lucy Andrews, petitioned the South Carolina Legislature to enslave her at the end of November 1860. Stranger still, she was wealthy and owned slaves ("Voluntary Slavery" 1).
* In the Nashville of the 1830s were "a number of well-to-do free Negroes who owned slaves, bought and sold them, and without compunction dealt in their own blood and nationality," in the words of Ira Stout, a longtime resident of the city. This host included Christopher Kit and "Old Porter." Kit owned property on Market Street, Porter possessed the corner of Broad and College Streets, and both had several slaves. Four other free blacks, Reuben Graham, Stephen Lytle, Dick Tate, and Buck McNary, owned not only carriages but also the slaves who drove them. As early as 1806 one "Old Black Bob" owned both a tavern on Market Street and the workers within ("Negroes Who Owned Negro Slaves" 4).
* Henry Todd of Darien, Georgia, was at one time the wealthiest black man in the state. He started out as a slave, but his master freed him in his will. Todd himself became a slaveowner and lost twenty slaves and some Confederate bonds at the end of the war. Nevertheless, he made a fortune through farming and the lumber business. As of 1882 he was worth $100,000 ("All Over the South" 26 Sep. 1882 4).
* Bob Parker, a black man who ran a line of dray carts in Columbus, Georgia, owned slaves including women and children. So did Joe Clark, also of Columbus. It was noted many years later that "[t]he free Negroes generally held themselves in high esteem and were respected by their white neighbors" ("Many Negroes Owned Slaves" 9).
* Sawmill operator Edward Parker died at his home on Fowl River in Alabama in May 1868 at age sixty-five, noted far and wide for his generosity. Born free, he amassed a fortune before the war. Like many a slaveowner of the era, he objected to the practice in principle, yet owned several, which, his obituary notes, "he always treated with kindness and indulgence." He thought it would have been better had the institution been gradually abolished, not ended abruptly ("Death of a Remarkable Negro" 1).
* As previously mentioned, some blacks in the North also owned slaves. On October 6, 1783, Samuel Stanton of Stonington, Connecticut, sold a female slave named Binar to a free black named Prince; in turn, Prince sold the woman to Isaac Denison in 1785 (Wilson 484). A free black man in Boston named Scipio purchased a slave named Margaret on November 28, 1724 (Wilson 484). As late as 1830, eight blacks in New York City owned seventeen slaves (Koger 1).

Many historians have endeavored to spin these uncomfortable facts. Prominently, Carter G. Woodson theorized in the 1920s that black slaveholding was actually a benevolent institution. According to this hypothesis, black masters purchased their own relatives to keep whites from owning them and sometimes with the express purpose of freeing them. Larry Koger mentions several documented cases of black slaveowners (and some white ones too) who freed slaves they purchased for humanitarian reasons.

However, unfortunately for this thesis, Koger's research indicates that most blacks bought slaves for exactly the same reason whites did: to make money from their labor and sometimes by selling them for a profit. In South Carolina, for example, black masters did sometimes purchase and emancipate relatives, but they also bought unrelated slaves whom they kept in bondage. It also appears most slaveowning blacks did not own relatives in the first place: "[T]he census of 1850 demonstrated that 83.1 percent of the Negro masters were mulattos, while nearly 90 percent of their slaves were of dark skin. Where was the kinship? Since mulattos primarily married mulattos, the black folk owned by light-skinned Afro-Americans were seldom kin and were overwhelmingly held as laborers. By and large, Negro slaveowners were darker copies of their white counterparts" (Koger xiii; 80-101).

Koger also turned up instances of black masters placing ads for the return of their runaway slaves, forcing rebellious laborers into jails or workhouses, having them flogged or sold for disobedience, and giving slaves to their children as inherited property (91-94). This is further illustrated by a seldom-quoted passage from Yankee traveler Frederick Law Olmsted concerning a conversation he had with a Louisiana black:

> He said ... that there were many free Negroes all about this region. Some of them were very rich. He pointed out to me three plantations, within twenty miles, owned by colored men. These bought black folks, he said, and had servants of their own. They were very bad masters, very hard and cruel—hadn't any feeling. "You might think, master, dat dey would be good to dar own nation; but dey is not. I will tell you de truth, massa; I know I'se got to answer; and it's a fact, dey is very bad masters, sar. I'd rather be a servant to any man in de world, dan to a brack man. If I was sold to a brack man, I'd drown myself. I would dat—I'd drown myself!—dough I shouldn't like to do dat nudder; but I wouldn't be sold to a colored master for anyting." (680)

In addition, there is evidence that black slaveowners weren't necessarily always kind even to bondsmen to whom they were actually related. Contemplate the strange case of Rose Petepher of New Bern, N.C., a free black woman who bought her runaway slave husband, Richard Gasken, from his master. They had many children whom they hired out just like slaves. A young man in the same neighborhood, Jacob, had a free black mother and a slave father, Jacob Sr. After assiduously saving their money, young Jacob and his mother bought the freedom of Jacob Sr. It sounds heartwarming, but one day Jacob Sr. reprimanded his son for misbehaving. Young Jacob retaliated by selling his father to a traveling slave merchant from up North named John Gildersleeve, who then sent the re-enslaved father to the Deep South. Young Jacob boasted that "the old man had gone to the corn fields about New Orleans where they might learn him some manners" (Wilson 485). In another case, a free black woman of Columbus, Georgia, named Dilsey Pope was not only married to a slave, she owned him outright and hired him out to others. One day in a fit of anger she sold him to Colonel Seaborn Jones. Remorseful, she later tried to repurchase him, but the new owner wouldn't sell (Wilson 487). Nelson Turner of Nashville made so much money as an undertaker that he bought his wife and stepdaughter from a white master, but "afterward got angry with his stepdaughter and sold her to a Negro trader." Jim Young, a free black of Wilson County,

Tennessee, bought his wife's freedom but then put her up as stakes in a poker game. He lost the game and his wife ("Negroes Who Owned Negro Slaves" 4).

Like many whites, slaveowners of color were reluctant to give up their workers as the Civil War came to an end. By 1864, when the writing on the wall clearly indicated the waning days of slavery, eighty-one blacks still refused to emancipate their 241 slaves in the city of Charleston, S.C., alone. The aftermath of the Civil War left many black plantation owners and former slaveholders financially devastated, as was the case with their white counterparts (Koger 192, 195-96). Loren Schweninger describes the loss of status suffered by these wealthy Southern blacks after the war: "Saddened by the passing of the old regime, disheartened by the loss of their privileged status, angered at being mistaken for former bondsmen, they ignored their business obligations during the 1870s and allowed their real estate holdings to evaporate" (48).

8

Strange Civil War Deaths

The chances of undergoing death by misadventure are increased exponentially in a war setting, where there are many opportunities for danger, accidents, exposure to the elements, and just plain foolishness, as these incidents demonstrate.

Confederate uniforms were generally gray or butternut. In the North, one could get away with wearing gray clothing since it was a common, neutral color—but civilians who ventured out of doors in butternut were likely to be considered, accurately or not, Southern sympathizers. The churchgoers in Mauckport, Indiana, were upset when a young lady named Miller showed up on July 10, 1864, wearing a butternut emblem. A Mrs. Timberlake was so offended that after the service she tried to forcibly remove it. The resulting fight was hardly appropriate for the location or the gender of the combatants. Miss Miller's escort, Henry Lohmire, tried to break up the fracas, but told Lieutenant Colonel John Timberlake of the 81st Indiana to mind his own business when he did the same.

Said the colonel, "You are nothing but a damned rebel anyhow."

Lohmire: "Don't say that again!"

The colonel: "You are a damned rebel ---- ----!" (Please fill in the blanks with your own imagination, as the newspapers don't report exactly what he said.)

Some witnesses said Timberlake punched Lohmire in the face and reached for his pocket in a threatening gesture. Lohmire was quicker on the draw and shot the colonel twice, killing him instantly ("Fatal Affray in Harrison County" 3).

History uncannily repeated itself only a couple of months later at Simpson Chapel, north of Bloomington, Indiana. A young woman had worn a butternut breastpin to church; offended lady peers tore it off. The women were prosecuted, and a compromise reached to the satisfaction of their parents. But the matter was far from settled. On September 11, as a Mr. Riddle and three Brown brothers exited after services, they were fired upon by others. Riddle was killed and all three Browns wounded ("A Sad Occurrence" 1). The papers did not explain in detail, but implied that the taking of the pin and the multiple shooting were connected. All this mayhem because women wore butternut in public.

John Thompson of Company I, 58th Illinois Volunteers, was held in the Exchange Barracks Prison in Louisville, Kentucky, for desertion. It appears that, unlike rebel prisoners, he had permission to leave the building. On December 2, 1864, he made a very poor sartorial choice: a butternut-colored suit. A sentry, thinking Thompson an escaping Confederate, shot him in the chest and killed him nearly instantly ("Shot by the Guard" 4).

In September 1868, long after the war, three "carpetbaggers" named Gallion, Young, and Courtney swore they would kill any man wearing gray at a religious meeting held in Hardin County, Tennessee. They found a man meeting that description named Worth Hardin. They were prevented from murdering him, but later shot his brother George eleven times on the highway, considering that good enough ("In Hardin County…" 2).

General Halbert Paine lay wounded at the Louisiana's Battle of Port Hudson in 1863. His assistant adjutant general offered $2,000 (modern equivalent, nearly $34,000) to anyone who would bring Paine a drink of water. One brave, or greedy, man took him up on the offer. Paine got his drink and lived to fight another day, but his water bearer was filled with Confederate lead ("While Gen. Paine lay wounded…"1).

Mr. E. Knapp Perry, a medical student of Warren County, Pennsylvania, got his draft notice in August 1863. He immediately became deranged and died soon after. The verdict was that he had been frightened to death ("Died of Draft Fright" 1).

A war correspondent using the superhero-like pseudonym Dr. Adonis wrote in mid-February 1864 of an incident among Federal soldiers stationed in Tennessee. Corporal Thomas Sharp of Company I, 38th Illinois, got drunk and thought it would be delightful to play a game of "Can I sneak past the picket?" Sharp had escaped serious injury at Fredericksburg, Perryville, Stone Gap, and Stones River, but he did not survive his own prank (Dr. Adonis 1).

Joseph Forsall, a private in Company D, 37th Illinois Regiment Infantry, exited the Louisville Theater on June 27, 1865, and demanded a glass of liquor at the next-door saloon. His request was denied since the military had ordered saloons not to sell alcohol to soldiers. Meanwhile, a black civilian customer was served. Miffed, Forsall reentered the theater and stormed into the box office. Mistakenly blaming the refusal on his race rather than military status, Forsall shouted, "I'll be damned if I'll live in a country where a Negro can have privileges denied to a white man!" He proved his point by stabbing himself in the heart ("His Name" 1; "The soldier that murdered himself…" 1). When the inquest was held right there in the theater, the late soldier was deemed insane ("Inquest No. 367" 1). A few years later, when the *Courier-Journal* recounted Forsall's dramatic exit from life's stage, some wag titled the story "A Scene Not on the Bills" ("Bloody Memories" 3).

On the morning of Friday, December 30, 1864, a woman got off a steamer from Norfolk, Virginia, onto the docks at Baltimore. She had a trunk so heavy that she enlisted a hackman named Stark to help her cart it to J. S. Palmatory's boardinghouse. The chatty but heavily veiled, black-clad lady—about forty years old, Stark estimated—told her helper that she was headed north and didn't need to rent a hotel room as she only planned to be in the city a few days. Stark carried the trunk up to her room on the boardinghouse's second floor.

The woman's behavior at Palmatory's establishment was strange, to say the least. She didn't leave her room, and at suppertime wanted only a cup of coffee. The servant who gave it to her said her head was muffled up. It was almost as though she didn't want anyone to see her face.

That night she announced that she would be leaving and rehired Mr. Stark to haul that trunk back downstairs, carry it to his wagon, and drive it to the train depot. At their destination, he took the box off his cart. The veiled lady said she had to make a few purchases, and would he mind waiting for her? Then she disappeared, leaving Stark at the depot with a big, mysterious trunk.

Not knowing what to do, Stark waited three hours, then hauled his burden back to his own house. Sometime the next day, December 31, people noticed that a bad smell was wafting from the trunk. A neighbor pried open the lid with a chisel, and bystanders suddenly had more than war news to discuss on New Year's Eve. The police arrived and took the contents to the "dead house," that is, the morgue.

The man was lying face down with his legs doubled under his stomach. The description given to the papers was luxuriously detailed: he was about forty years old; 5 feet, 5 inches tall; had light brown hair, a sandy moustache and beard, but no side whiskers; was wearing blue woolen socks and black cassimere pants; his pockets held a pencil, a comb, and a penknife, but no clues as to his identity. The police assumed he was a murder victim although there were no marks of violence on his body. Some thought he had been placed in the box to suffocate, while others thought he was stuffed in after death.

There were two clues. The trunk had tiny holes drilled in one side, and the veiled woman had applied for a wartime pass to travel from Norfolk to Baltimore under the name Miss Linder. The mystery remained for only about an hour. At 9 p.m. the veiled woman turned herself in at the police station.

She was in fact Mary Louise Linder, age thirty-seven, a "woman of ill repute" who lived in Norfolk. She said the man was Samuel Freeborn of Company M, 20th New York cavalry, and that she had been hiding him alive at her house for the past three months.

What was Freeborn doing in a trunk? He had gotten an enlistment bonus of $1,000 and then deserted. The pair plotted to mail him off to Canada where she could rejoin him and enjoy Uncle Sam's misplaced generosity. After all, government officials wouldn't closely examine a woman's clothing trunk—would they? Freeborn had drilled the holes in the box himself, but they were too small and did not permit sufficient oxygen. He suffocated while in hiding. A reporter who examined the trunk later said the openings would not have allowed in enough air to keep a rat alive.

So there was poor Miss Linder, stuck in Baltimore with a dead man in a trunk and precious few resources for getting rid of him. Her plan had been to abandon the trunk to whomever found it, or perhaps send it off to Chicago. But then her conscience preyed upon her, and she gave herself up ("Mysterious Affair in Baltimore" 1).

Miss Linder went on trial in Norfolk a few weeks later. It ended on January 7, 1865. She was found guilty, not of murder or manslaughter, but of aiding and abetting a deserter. The scheme she and her lover had cooked up to defraud the government cost Freeborn his life and cost her two years in prison at hard labor and a $500 fine. She considered herself lucky, as she thought she would hang ("Norfolk: The Great Trunk Tragedy" 1).

Most soldiers in wartime have the understandable attitude that they would like to survive the experience. Not so Edward Rogers of the 1st Vermont Cavalry, who entered the military wishing to get killed. He even violated orders hoping that death would be his portion. Somehow he lived through it all. After his discharge, he ate arsenic in Georgia, Vermont, on August 19, 1865, and thereby relieved his disappointment. No word as to why Rogers had such an insatiable death wish ("A young man..." 4). He recently had been married, but let's not entertain a possible post hoc fallacy.

The Battle of Blue Mills Landing took place in Clay County, Missouri, on September 17, 1861. A soldier named Schelling of the 3rd Iowa Volunteers was found standing like a statue on the battlefield, seemingly oblivious to his surroundings, near a cannon, and with a rammer in his hand. He was taken unconscious to Kansas City. Doctors were puzzled. He had no visible injuries, no effects of concussion. The pupils of his eyes were normal, but he could eat and drink only if force-fed. He remained in this comatose state for seventeen days, then died, but what of no one ever figured out. The leading theory was that the sound of firing on the battlefield frightened him into a slow death ("Singular Death from Terror" 1).

Union veteran Jacob Koch decided to end his life in Philadelphia on March 29, 1866, in this fashion. He loaded a child's toy cannon with real gunpowder and placed a marble in its barrel. Then he put the barrel in his mouth and touched off the powder. "The discharge that followed sent the marble through his skull," observed a local paper, "while the powder shattered his cranium into atoms.... The whole cerebellum was shattered to pieces and the brain itself was spattered about the room" ("Singular Suicide" 4). The toy cannon was every bit as efficient as a real one.

In the winter of 1864, the Union officers who occupied Vicksburg found themselves with little to do. One night in a hall on Washington Street, Captains Jessup and Sholes got intoxicated and deemed a game of William Tell just the thing to stave off boredom. Sholes staggered ten paces, placed a tin cup on his head, and challenged Jessup to shoot it off. Jessup didn't think this was such a great idea, but Sholes insisted. In that split second just before Jessup fired, Sholes stood up a little straighter. The aftermath was reported in the nation's newspaper dispatches ("A Fatal Spree Among Officers" 2).

Confederate veteran Allan Cogsdell rode to Rutherfordton, North Carolina, one day in April 1902 and handed his old army pistol to a gunsmith with instructions that it must be in perfect working condition by June 9. Afterward, Mr. Cogsdell set to work putting his affairs in order, which including having the following notice printed on cards which he distributed to hundreds of friends and acquaintances: "The pleasure of your company is respectfully requested by the undersigned at his suicide, which will take place at high noon, June 10, 1902, in his residence, Colfax Township, near Rutherfordton. Dinner will be served promptly at 11 o'clock, and will last exactly one hour, the undersigned acting as host to his friends for the last time. On the stroke of 12 he will blow out his brains in the presence of the assembled guests. No flowers. R.S.V.P." ("Come See Me Die" 4).

Naturally, recipients asked Cogsdell whether the invitation was on the level, and he affirmed with steely resolve that it was. But on the appointed day Cogsdell changed his mind for undisclosed reasons ("Cogdell [*sic*] Doesn't Suicide" 5).

Ohio Senator Clement Vallandigham made a name for himself as leader of the Peace Democrats, a faction determined to pressure Lincoln into ending the war by any means possible. Northerners who wanted to fight to a conclusion had another name for Vallandigham's movement: the Copperheads. The president retaliated with force, using what some might deem Constitutionally dubious means. He had the senator banished to the South. Vallandigham migrated to Canada, where he continued being a thorn in the administration's side. He moved back to Ohio after the war and became an attorney.

June 16, 1871, found Vallandigham in court defending Thomas McGehan, accused of shooting Tom Myers in a fight. The former chief of Copperheads argued that Myers had shot himself accidentally while pulling his pistol from his pocket. Vallandigham demonstrated to his co-attorneys how he planned to act out his defense of McGehan by recreating Myers's movements. Fortunately, his simulation occurred away from the jury. He knelt, as had Myers, and pulled a loaded pistol from his right pocket. He cocked it and held it in the same position he theorized Myers had. Suddenly the gun went off, and the attorney had a self-inflicted wound that terminated fatally the next day. His client faced a hung jury, then a mistrial, and was acquitted at a third trial (Klement 309-10). His happy ending was temporary, however, as the "notorious desperado" was murdered himself by an unknown assailant in his Basin Street saloon in Hamilton, Ohio, on June 14, 1875 ("Cincinnati" 1).

Anything absurd can become absurder. Vallandigham died trying to replicate an accidental shooting, and two weeks after his death, a German in Hamilton accidentally shot himself trying to imitate Vallandigham's imitation ("Another Vallandigham Accident" 1). He was reportedly recovering a month later ("The *Cincinnati Commercial*" 3).

9
Bivouac of the Dead

What do you do with the bodies of dozens—perhaps hundreds, or tens of thousands—of people, mostly out-of-towners, who died suddenly and violently in your community? Our ancestors who lived near Civil War battlefields confronted that daunting chore. These stories concern the disposal of soldiers' remains, with solutions ranging from respectful to very much the reverse.

In 1862, a coffin was shipped to Gray, Maine. Amos and Sarah Colley, who had paid the government for the delivery, thought it contained their Union soldier son Charles, who died of wounds received on August 9 at the Battle of Cedar Mountain in Virginia. Instead, it held a Confederate with no identification except his gray uniform. What to do with the anonymous soldier? The War Department had no provisions for a wrong delivery and the Colleys couldn't afford to send the body back. They chose to bury him in the grave prepared for their son in the town cemetery. Later, local women paid for a tombstone reading, "Unknown. A soldier of the late war. Died 1862. Erected by the Ladies of Gray." Every Memorial Day, a small Confederate flag is left on his grave ("The Unknown Confederate Solider").

On March 3, 1864, Mr. John Joblin of Zanesville, Ohio, received a large metallic receptacle in the mail, what Poe would have called an "oblong box," disturbingly very like a coffin. But no one was certain, as there were no accompanying letters, cards, or other forms of explanation. After opening the lid, no doubt with trembling hands, he found inside his half-brother Lieutenant Thomas Hopes, lately stationed at Vicksburg. The local paper said, "The body is in a remarkably good state of preservation" ("Singular Circumstance" 3).

One especially horrifying fact about Civil War battles is how long it often took to clean up the mess afterward. The Battle of Wilson's Creek was fought near Springfield, Missouri, on August 10, 1861; a *Cincinnati Gazette* correspondent noted that almost two weeks later, an estimated seventy-five to one hundred Union soldiers still lay strewn about. The writer did not spare disagreeable details:

> Those who fell in the hollows, or where the ground was soft, have been hid from view. The stench arising from the field is not as overpowering as might be supposed.... In several instances, the visitor can distinctly see where wounded men have dragged themselves from the place where they fell, to the shade afforded by the few scrubby oak

> bushes in the field, and there, with the crimson tide of life ebbing away, and no kind hand to administer so trifling a thing as a cup of water, for the want of which they were famishing, they laid them down to die. ("The Battlefield a Fortnight…" 4)

The Battle of Perryville, Kentucky (also called the Battle of Chaplin Hills), took place on a chilly October 8, 1862. A Union soldier using the pen name Lochiel gruesomely described the condition of the dead after it was much safer to observe them. Wounded Illinois soldiers burned to death, along with a flock of sheep, after exploding shells set off a grass fire. While some burned, others froze, dying from exposure to the elements on that frigid autumn night. The Union Army won the battle and had the luxury of burying its casualties on October 9 and 10. However, the retreating Confederates had no time for such niceties and fled with the conviction that disposal of the Southern dead was now someone else's problem. Lochiel estimated that he saw three thousand rebels "lying mangled and torn, festering and putrefying, and the hogs devouring them!" Residents of Perryville buried as many as they could, fearing a possible pestilence, but they missed some who crawled to die with a little privacy in hiding places—behind logs, in ravines, under cover of bushes. Lochiel opined that some would not be found until angel Gabriel blew the final trumpet, and perhaps he was right (Lochiel 3).

It appears that properly revering the noble dead at Perryville was not a top priority. An entire year after the campaign, the Boyle County court appointed J. C. Barkley and Jordan Peter to examine the battlefield's condition. On October 19, 1863, they reported that some graves were so damaged that the bones within were visible—and these were

"Battlefield of Gettysburg. Bodies of dead Federal soldiers on the field of the first day's battle" by Timothy O'Sullivan. (*Library of Congress Prints and Photographs Division*)

the Yankee soldiers who allegedly had been given a "good" burial as opposed to the Confederates just left lying around. The local paper, the *Danville Tribune*, proposed that when the state legislature met in December, it should pass a bill to erect a monument on the field ("Perryville Battlefield" 2). But in the meanwhile, admonished the press, cover up those exposed bones!

Gettysburg was fought, famously, from July 1–3, 1863, just before Independence Day. A month later, the area was not yet cleared of all the dead, and this at the height of summer. For some reason, the military ordered corpse removal work halted for all of August and September; perhaps the weather was just too hot for such intensive labor. Nevertheless, bodies on the outskirts were removed. Some parents traveled up to 1,000 miles to collect these remains. A journalist for the *Philadelphia Ledger* complained about the humanitarian practice in a letter printed on August 8, claiming it was better to let soldiers stay buried where they were slain. He speculated that it would be cheaper on the families just to raise a monument in their local cemetery than journey so far to take the body home. Dragging all those corpses around was bad for "the health and morals of the living," the latter because it made people too comfortable with the terrors of death, he thought; the "unwise and unnatural familiarity with death and dead bodies" could only breed disrespect in the long run. And what good could it do to have all these coffins lying around in public view at the nation's train depots, he wondered. "The blessedness of letting the soldier lie undisturbed in the grave where soldiers have laid him is not enough considered," the *Philadelphia Ledger*'s writer concluded ("The Removal of the Dead" 1). However, he was overlooking something. All those bodies had to be removed from Gettysburg as soon as possible so the president could deliver some short and inconsequential little address there on November 19.

The Battle of Chickamauga was fought in Georgia from September 18–20, 1863. Yet months later, in January 1864, the *Mobile Advertiser* reported that "heaps" of unburied Union soldiers remained on the field ("The *Mobile Advertiser* says..." 1). A visitor to the site in July 1865, after the war's end, said both North and South had been buried hastily in shallow mounds, and the unlovely attractions for the sightseer included two sun-bleached skulls—one a home to a nest of industrious wasps—plus two pairs of boots full of foot bones ("A visitor to the battlefield..." 3).

Virginia's Battle of the Wilderness took place from May 5–7, 1864. An officer who visited the location six weeks later declared that at least 15,000 Union dead and many more Confederates lay around in open view to impress the spectator. To put that number in perspective, it would be the entire population of some modern U.S. cities or counties. "[I]magination in its wildest fancies cannot begin to paint the spectacle," he elegantly said ("The Unburied Dead in the Wilderness" 1).

As late as April 1867, Dr. John M. Johnson, a former member of the Kentucky Senate, noted that the Confederate dead near Atlanta still had not been buried, and instead were "lying everywhere ... upon the top of the ground with not a handful of earth or a leaf above them, bleaching and ghastly skeletons" ("Burial of the Confederate Dead" 1). Perhaps the locals were used to it by then.

Suppose it is 1865 and one of your relatives was a soldier buried on a battlefield. You wanted to have him exhumed and sent home for burial, as in the Gettysburg example above. What was the proper process? The government directed in October 1865 that the seeker must make an affidavit before a notary public or justice of the peace

Dead Confederate artillerymen at Antietam. (*Library of Congress Prints and Photographs Division*)

affirming authorization to take the body. The applicant also must furnish the soldier's company and regiment. The paperwork went to the office of the quartermaster who, after processing the forms, would receive an official exhumation order. The government provided information about the internment and permission to disinter for free, but the expense of digging and shipping fell upon the relatives. "It is essential," added the order, though probably unnecessarily, "that a body be so prepared as to prevent any unpleasant odor, which can be done by means of disinfecting powder, or by sealing it in a metallic or airtight deodorizing case" ("How to Obtain the Bodies" 1).

No doubt many people bypassed all this red tape by furtively visiting battlefields with a shovel, a box, and a round-trip train ticket. To illustrate: around November 1865, a man went to Petersburg, Virginia, to collect a brother who had died in battle there in March. He gathered the bones, then found that a coffin and transportation would cost more than he could afford. He carried the remains home in a carpetbag ("Corpse in a Carpetbag" 1).

Some dead soldiers did get prompt burials—but occasionally not very good ones, interments sometimes having been performed hastily out of necessity. Although no battles were fought at Bowling Green, Kentucky, a number of rebel soldiers stationed nearby died of illness and injury. One resident estimated that between 3,000 and 4,000 Southern fighters died there, and the number would have been greater if so many of the sick and dying had not been shipped to Nashville. "The dead were so carelessly buried that the stench arising from the graveyards is horrible," wrote a war correspondent in March 1862, "and a committee has waited on the Kentucky Legislature, praying the appointment of a sanitary commission, to make an examination and report what can be done to avert a pestilence" ("Bowling Green" 1; "Immediately in and around Bowling Green..." 2). The writer concluded that if action were not taken before the advent of warm weather, Bowling Green would become uninhabitable.

The Kentucky Legislature must have had other things to do, because a full week later the air around Bowling Green was laden with terror and bad smells. The estimated number of Confederates half-buried in the vicinity had risen to a possible 6,000. But as a balm for the locals' fears, a *Louisville Journal* correspondent reassured them that the rebels decaying *al fresco* could not start a plague. "Let not our fellow-citizens of Bowling Green idly dream that the miserably buried bodies of the rebels can have anything to do in the production of pestilence. *There is no instance in human history where a pestilence has been produced by the decay of animal matter*" ("Bowling Green: The Fears of Pestilence" 2). Italics are his.

An aside: Today we have professional body removal services and crime scene cleaners, but the reader might be wondering how the people of the 1860s purified the vicinity after a body was removed. They used the same chemicals used to clean up during the disposal of defunct animals: they liberally sprinkled a homemade disinfectant created by mixing one pound of chloride of lime with one gallon of water. It was very effective, had the additional advantage of being cheap. Users were cautioned to bathe thoroughly and destroy their clothing afterward ("Cattle Plague" 1).

Then there was the postbellum problem of removing soldiers from battlefield tombs, or even mass graves, and moving them to military cemeteries. The labor this entailed may be gleaned from an advertisement placed in the *Louisville Journal* of October 31, 1865, in which the government quartermaster asked would-be exhumers and re-inhumers to offer bids for performing their ghastly tasks in and around the city. The winner was expected to furnish stained and varnished coffins; remove and carry bodies in "light, covered spring wagons"; cover the coffins in American flags; dig graves not less than 5 feet deep, complete with a vault; and erect wooden headboards including the soldier's name, rank, company, regiment, place of birth and date of death—all neatly painted ("Proposals for Burial of Deceased Soldiers" 2).

Sometime those employed in disinterring soldiers got shocking surprises. For example, Mr. Berry of the 7th Tennessee Infantry was killed at Fredericksburg, Virginia, in December 1862. Immediately afterward, he was placed in a metallic casket which, for reasons that do not appear in the record, remained unburied for a year. At last, for reasons equally arcane, someone finally buried it. In March 1866, a friend dug up Berry's casket and took it through Lebanon, Tennessee, *en route* to his final resting place in Sumner County. When folks opened the lid, because that is the sort of thing people were curious about in those days, they found Berry perfectly preserved. His iron casket got the credit ("The *Lebanon* [TN] *Herald* notices..." 3).

The steamboat *Sultana*, carrying mostly Union soldiers on their way home, exploded near Memphis on April 27, 1865, killing 1,168. Some of that multitude was buried at Fort Pickering. They were exhumed in February 1867 for reinterment in Memphis National Cemetery. When the dead were brought back into the sunlight, workers were amazed to find that "the bodies had undergone little or no change, the color and texture of the skin being

A line of Confederate soldiers awaiting burial. (*Library of Congress Prints and Photographs Division*)

Burial of the Union dead at Fredericksburg. Photo taken May 19 or 20, 1864, long after the battle. (*Library of Congress Prints and Photographs Division*)

preserved almost intact, while other bodies, buried before and after in the same ground, had yielded to the natural decay of the grave" ("Bodies of victims lost by the explosion…" 2). It was thought that the trauma of the explosion had somehow preserved their corpses.

Major Wainwright was tasked with removing Union soldiers' bodies from Resaca, Georgia, to be reburied in Chattanooga. In June 1866, his men unearthed one corpse shot through the head, but which had tiny feet. Their suspicions aflame, they took a closer look and found that the body was that of a woman who had enlisted in disguise. Whoever she really was, she went by the name "Private Charles Janghaus" of Company E, 6th Missouri Volunteers ("Strange Incident" 3). Similarly, in September 1866, gravediggers searching for Union soldiers at the site of the notorious Battle of the Crater near Petersburg, Virginia, also found a woman who had masqueraded as a man that she might join the service. A news report bizarrely observed that she "was in an excellent state of preservation—the bust, especially, was perfect" ("The *Petersburg Index* says…" September 15, 1866 1).

In July 1867, Union soldiers killed near Egypt Station, Mississippi, were exhumed. One was found to have pockets full of stolen silver spoons. The rightful owner was located, and the plunder returned ("The Aberdeen [MS] *Examiner…*" 2).

A soldier who died at Chickamauga was exhumed in July 1871. Not only was he well-preserved, but observers noted that though he had been clean-shaven when buried, he now sported a moustache an inch in thickness ("The *Newnan* [GA] *Defender* says…" 2).

Camp Douglas in Chicago was a camp for Confederate prisoners of war. Those who died there were interred near Lincoln Park, but later moved to Oak Woods Cemetery. One unearthed coffin bore no name. Could the bones within be identified? When the lid was opened, officials were surprised to see a skeleton wrapped in a Mexican poncho, of all things. But through this unlikely garment he was recognized as the brother-in-law of a Texan who had sent it as a gift ("Camp Douglas" 3).

Workers exhuming Federal soldiers at Glasgow, Kentucky, in August 1867 opened a coffin lid and found the tenant in a distorted position and with his pillow on his chest. As if being seriously wounded in the war weren't bad enough, the poor fellow had been mistaken for dead and buried alive ("Buried Alive" 2).

An honest Irishman was hired in December 1867 to move war victims from St. Louis's Wesleyan Cemetery. When hoisting coffins, he found they were lighter than expected and sounded hollow. An inspection disclosed that no bodies ever had been placed in them, just planks or wooden blocks. Unscrupulous undertakers had charged to bury the bodies, and then sold them to medical schools surreptitiously for dissection purposes, taking the phrase "war profiteer" to a grotesque level ("Horrible Fraud" 3).

Henry Wirz achieved lasting infamy as the commandant at Georgia's Andersonville prison camp. Hanged for overseeing atrocities against Union prisoners on November 10, 1865, he was buried in the Washington Arsenal prison yard. He was unearthed in late February 1869, with President's Johnson's permission, so family members could rebury him in a less punitive location. His excavators made the interesting discovery that Wirz had been consigned to the earth stark naked, and his skull, right arm, and two neckbones were missing. Army surgeons had removed the vertebrae and the arm, which were on display at the National Medical Museum. Who took the skull? No one admitted to it, but fortunately, at least the thief left behind Wirz's empty head with face, hair, and beard intact, not unlike a deflated basketball. Fortunately, because someone had implored the undertaker to snip off a lock of Wirz's hair ("Wirz" 3).

Right: Reporters and police awaiting the execution of Andersonville's Henry Wirz. (*Library of Congress Prints and Photographs Division*)

Below: The hangman adjusts Wirz's noose. (*Library of Congress Prints and Photographs Division*)

The process of moving bodies to federal cemeteries was usually performed with the respect and solemn dignity becoming the occasion. But not always! A *New York World* correspondent writing from Fayette County, Tennessee, in March 1867 was scandalized by the cavalier fashion adopted by laborers. "They threw out the dirt with spades until they came to the box which contained the dead." So far so good. But then the workers used their spades to break the lid; beheaded soldiers and flung the skulls out of the graves; then cut the bodies in half at the pelvis and tossed up the two halves; then cut off the legs at the knee joints and threw the legs out; then pitched out the feet. All this dissecting and bisecting was performed with their sharpened spades. Evidently this was considered less trouble than simply removing an intact body. When the workmen were finished, they moved on to the next grave, probably while whistling popular songs of the day such as "The Man on the Flying Trapeze" and "Johnny, I Hardly Knew Ye," while others collected the discarded parts and placed them in boxes. The offended spectator concluded, "Now I think that, unless we get men who will treat dead bodies as they should, it were better to have the bodies sleep where they are" ("Shameful If True" 2).

In August 1867, a detail of men was set in charge of removing thirty Federal soldiers from their resting places near Glasgow, Kentucky, for reinterment in a national cemetery at Tompkinsville. "It was a singularly disgusting spectacle to witness the mode of disinterment pursued by the squad engaged in the work," wrote an eyewitness ("Horrible Inhumanity" 2). What he meant by that: the contents of burst coffins were all

The gruesome process of collecting and burying long-dead soldiers. (*Library of Congress Prints and Photographs Division*)

shoveled together and dumped promiscuously into new coffins, thus hopelessly mixing the remains.

In a third case from January 1869, the government agent given the duty to exhume and rebury soldiers in a national cemetery in east Tennessee was accused of planting horse skeletons along with the humans ("It is complained that the remains..." 2).

In 1884, a reminiscing soldier, B. B. Taylor, enthralled his readers by telling all about that unseasonably warm December day he was strolling in a Chattanooga cemetery between battles. No doubt Taylor was meditating on mortality and the mysteries of life and death when his thoughts were rudely interrupted by seemingly disembodied voices shouting things like "Clubs are trumps!" and "The ace of hearts takes the trick!" The voices echoed from a crypt with an open door. Taylor found soldiers using a casket as a card table and three others as chairs. The trio of gamblers was in a sorry state of disrepair. As the writer noted, "There were only four sound arms and five legs to divide among them" ("Playing Cards in a Cemetery Vault" 13).

In March 1862—about nine months after the First Battle of Bull Run, and five months before the Second—a *Philadelphia Press* journalist signing his name "J.R.Y." described how once-occupied Centreville, near the battlefield, presently appeared. After rhapsodizing over the grand weather, the "coy and bracing" breezes, and the gorgeous mountain scenery, he observed abandoned clues revealing soldiers' hasty departure: shattered cookware, torn cartridge boxes, haversacks, hats, shoes (for human or horse) and pipes. Then came the most undeniable evidence of the great battle that had taken place in that splendid land. First, the skeletons of horses, then shattered trees, and finally a mass grave full of Union soldiers. "I am sorry to say that, from what I heard, all the stories of the indignities heaped upon their remains—the plunder and rapine—were true" ("The Battlefield of Bull Run" 1).

What did J.R.Y. mean by "indignities"? According to a *Cincinnati Gazette* correspondent writing at the same time, a lieutenant colonel of the 3rd New Jersey regiment charged that rebel soldiers had mutilated their dead Union counterparts after the battle. The officer said that in one abandoned rebel tent he saw a skull with "Sic semper tyrannis" inscribed on it, and found other skulls used as ladles and bones used as pipes. A local resident named Bringle professed that he had seen Southern soldiers unearthing dead Federals, decapitating them, and parading around with their heads skewered on bayonets ("A special to the *Cincinnati Gazette*..." 3). A *New York World* writer said that Manassas resident Mrs. Butler told him that she witnessed Confederates digging up nine dead Union soldiers on her property, boiling the flesh from their bodies, and distributing the bones as souvenirs. The odor was so bad, said Mrs. Butler, that her family had to abandon their house. According to the *World* man, Northern soldiers found bits of polished human bones around the battlefield months after the fight ("Mutilation of Our Dead" 4).

Harper's Weekly of June 7, 1862, accused the rebels of even worse. The newspaper included an illustration featuring six pieces of furniture allegedly manufactured by Southerners from the bodies of dead Yanks. These included a skull goblet, a jawbone paperweight, a necklace of teeth, a cake basket fashioned from ribs, and (most ambitiously, most preposterously) a writing desk made from an entire skeleton (Garrison *Civil War Curiosities* 243).

Were these outlandish stories of corpse desecration true? Perhaps, but one should take them with not with a grain of salt, but a salt mine. In any war, it is imperative to make the opposing side look as inhuman, if not demonic, as possible. Considering that none of this folk art turned up later, it is a pretty safe bet the charges were all propaganda. The *Harper's* artist's unflattering hatchet-faced rendition of a Southern woman wearing a head wreath made of teeth is rather a giveaway. There was noticeably little talk of such postmortem atrocities *after* the war.

Perhaps the best hope a dying soldier had for the dispensation of his remains was to be embalmed and sent to his family. It was expensive, but the process was used often enough that the war is considered a major catalyst in making it well-known and accepted among the masses. A correspondent for the *London Times* writing from Virginia's Pamunkey River on June 15, 1862, saw a sign marked "Drs. Brown and Alexander, Government Embalmers." The inquisitive journalist saw four bodies the doctors had been laboring over, all dead of fever rather than war injuries, and was told that the embalming fluid included gypsum, which would keep the recipients in top-drawer condition for years—perhaps forever. The families of enlisted men were charged $22.00 (slightly more than $450 when translated into modern currency) while officers went for $50.00 (a bit over $1,000). It appears that all bodies got the same treatment, so officers were charged more strictly because of their higher rank and for no other reason. The British writer said that after the process, soldiers were placed in zinc-lined coffins, given a bundle of hay as a pillow, and shipped home ("The Embalming Business in the Army" 1). In February 1864, a doctor at Washington, D.C.'s Armory Square Hospital estimated that the cost of embalming and packing a body was $7, so it appears the professionals were overcharging ("Embalming" 4).

Northern soldiers had to flee the site of the Battle of the Wilderness without burying their dead. This was the scene several months later. (*Library of Congress Prints and Photographs Division*)

A journalist described the "easily comprehended" process while visiting City Point, Virginia, in November 1864. Blood was drawn from an incision in the neck, and then embalming fluid was pumped into the body via a rubber tube attached to a needle in the femoral artery. Unlike the embalmers who spoke with the British journalist quoted above, these were coy as to the secret ingredients of the fluid, but most observers agreed that good old-fashioned arsenic was the main component. If performed correctly, the subject's face should look natural though perhaps darker than in life. If a body were not embalmed within three days of its demise in the summertime, little could be done to preserve it. The anonymous reporter disapproved of the very concept of embalming: "Upon the desirableness of having a friend's body embalmed and taken home, I am strongly in the negative. If he falls in fighting for a sacred principle, his body will help consecrate the soil and make it truly sacred dust" ("How Bodies Are Embalmed" 1). Considering that the writer was described as "a correspondent of a Philadelphia paper," one wonders if he was the same *Philadelphia Press* journalist who was so opposed to exhuming soldiers in battlefield graves for reburial in their hometowns, as related above.

The steamboat *Ella Faber* sailed from Nashville in February 1863, bringing with her several sick or wounded Union soldiers. *En route*, four died. The captain ordered the bodies nailed up in boxes and wanted to have them buried in towns the ship passed. But Major Kelley insisted they be delivered to friends and relatives. When the ship arrived at its destination, Louisville, no grief-stricken next of kin stepped forth to claim the soldiers. No one knew what to do with them, so the boxes were turned over to the city wharfmaster as if they contained spoiling fruit. Likely they were buried at city expense. "Such neglect on the part of the proper authorities is highly reprehensible," commented the *Louisville Journal* ("Injustice to the Dead" 3). But it happened again on August 10, when the crew of the *Tycoon* had no choice but to dump at the Louisville docks five soldiers exuding "an intolerable stench," who had died on the trip from Vicksburg ("Barbarous" 3).

There is no event so tragic that someone won't try to make money from it. A Washington, D.C., attorney was arrested in April 1863 for pulling the following heartless scam: he would write to the friends of a dead soldier and offer to send the body—for a modest financial consideration, of course. When he got the cash, he would send just any old body he could scrape up ("A lawyer has been arrested..." 1).

By late June 1864, so many rebel soldiers died of illness at Richmond, Virginia, hospitals, that Hollywood Cemetery ran out of room for them. One witness saw twenty-five green pine coffins on the grounds, fastened with only one nail on each end—presumably the war was causing a shortage in metal necessary for manufacturing nails. The warmth of the summer sun and natural decaying processes of the human bodies ensured that the barely closed lids didn't stay shut for long. They creaked open, "exposing the putrescent bodies to full view, emitting sickening odors and attracting swarms of flies" ("A late Richmond paper says..." 1).

But even these deceased were lucky compared to others. Five years later, in late March 1869, Confederate veteran J. H. Allen, formerly of the 15th Virginia Regiment, heard rumors that atrocious vandalism had been perpetrated against his long-gone comrades in the graveyard at Fort Harrison in Henrico. Allen investigated, and 400 yards from the fort he found at least fifty skeletons' worth of bones scattered in a field, and "four times the number" in the bushes. Dogs had been gnawing on this unholy feast, and

Dr. Bunnell's embalming shack near Fredericksburg, *circa* 1864. (*Library of Congress Prints and Photographs Division*)

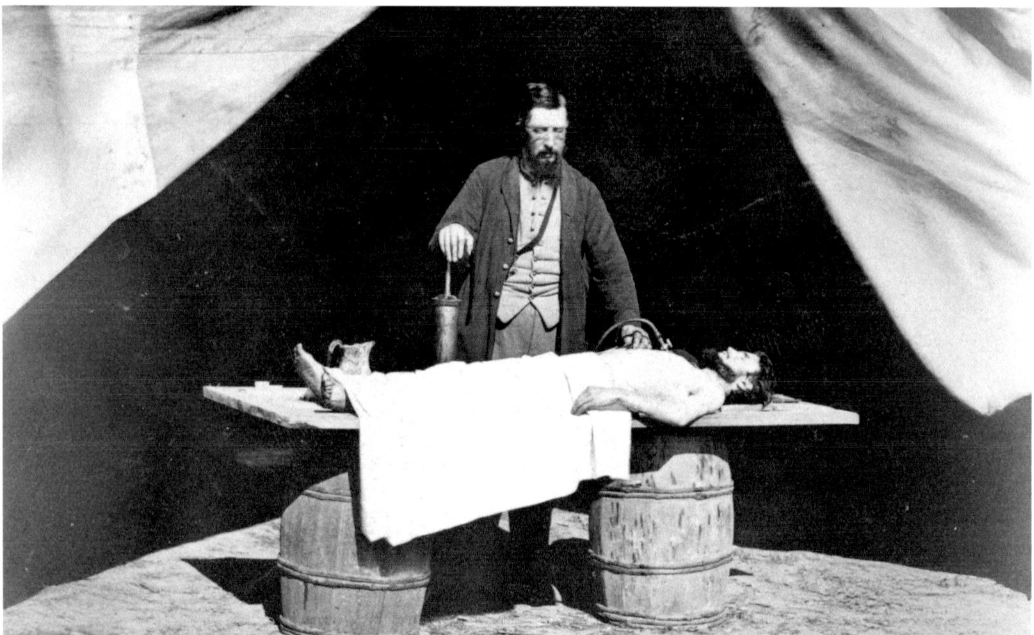

Photo of Dr. Richard Burr, embalmer for Army of the James, plying his trade *circa* 1863–1865. (*Library of Congress Prints and Photographs Division*)

two piles of bones had been set on fire. He said he made this discovery on April 1 ("A Shocking Statement" 1). Perhaps some readers of the *Richmond Dispatch* thought it an April Fool's Day joke in atrocious taste, but a party of investigators went to Fort Harrison on April 9 and found the accusation only too true. They reported that some bodies appeared to have been uncovered by rain, others by dogs, and still others plowed up and tossed in heaps by farmers. To prove their point, they hauled two cartloads of remains to Richmond, which were buried with the unknown Confederate dead in Hollywood Cemetery ("The Human Jackals of Fort Harrison" 1). Presumably all was set right later.

The body of a Union soldier arrived at Indianapolis on November 28, 1864, and was driven to the cemetery by sorrowing friends and relatives who discovered, when they got to the location, that the sexton had neglected to dig a grave. This subtracted somewhat from the dignity of the occasion, as did the resulting fight which ended with one of the burial party being shot in the thigh ("A Singular Occurrence" 1).

The Soldiers' Cemetery in Nashville was in scandalous condition by September 1866, when it was reported that the graves were only 2.5 feet deep. But the average coffin was 16 inches high, so once it was placed in a plot and dirt shoveled over it, only slightly more than 1 foot of earth separated the lid from the surface. A city paper complained, "The stench arising from these shallow graves is a great annoyance to the surrounding neighborhood" ("Burial of Soldiers" 3).

"Bloody Bill" Anderson, much-feared Confederate guerrilla, was shot at Albany, Missouri, on October 26, 1864. His body foreshadowed the fate suffered by so many Wild West outlaws in the years to come. It was paraded through the streets of Richmond, Missouri, then photographed, and the pictures sold to eager Northern sympathizers who wanted proof Anderson was dead. Here is how one appreciative spectator described the likeness: "His mouth is partially open, disclosing his front teeth, and imparting to the expression a half-ironic, hideous grin." He was buried decently near Richmond, which not everyone thought he deserved; one of his begrudging captors called it "a respect due not to him, but to ourselves and humanity" ("Bill Anderson in Mortuis" 1). A human scalp was found tied to Anderson's horse, but Union soldiers avenged that atrocity by cutting off one of his fingers and swiping a ring ("Anderson—His Burial..." 1).

Anderson's right-hand man Bill Stuart was also killed a few weeks later, shot three times by cattleman W. H. Burford at Franklin, Missouri, on November 17. In mid-December, it was reported that his body too had been photographed for souvenir collectors. Both postmortem portraits can readily be found on the internet. Mr. Anderson's face wears that expression we all have when we finally get a joke; as for Mr. Stuart, contemporary accounts inform us that one bullet hit him over the eye ("Bill Stuart's Photograph" 1) and the ambrotype reveals a sizable hole in exactly that location. He also has blood oozing from his mouth, which some artiste of the past accentuated with red tinting.

Union Colonel Ulric Dahlgren was shot near Richmond during a night raid on March 2, 1864. First, the rebels put his body on public display in the city; then they removed his uniform and dressed him a gray shirt and pants; then removed his spiffy cork leg and gave it to amputee J. N. Ballard of Mosby's Rangers; then stole his watch and his ring, including the finger; then they buried Dahlgren in an unmarked grave (Garrison *Civil War Curiosities* 36, 209; Garrison *Treasury of Civil War Tales* 177). Union spy Elizabeth Van Lew was so upset by this corpse desecration that she risked blowing her

Bloody Bill Anderson, deceased. Photo taken October 27, 1864, in Richmond, MO. (*Public Domain. Wikimedia*)

cover by having his body secretly exhumed and buried in a private location 10 miles from town (Suhr).

Colonel Melvin Grigsby recounted a time when prisoners of war found ways to turn the dead to financial advantage. A total of 3,000 Federal troops were captured in May 1864 at Plymouth, N.C., and taken to Andersonville prison. They were flush with money, having just received their veterans' bounty and new uniforms.

By this point in the war, the Confederacy was so impoverished that gambling was done for the paltriest sums and hucksters bartered for goods rather than selling them. Meanwhile, Confederate officers smuggled such items as eggs and tobacco into the jail to sell to their comparatively wealthy prisoners. Since prisoners carried sick or dying fellow POWs to the institution's hospital, a chance to go outside was worth considerable money because stretcher bearers had the chance to purchase smuggled goods from, or sell them to, their captors.

Inevitably, dead men became valuable commodities, especially in summer months when fifty to 120 passed away daily. Occasional storms also would increase the inventory. But suppose several corpses had to be borne away at the same time, which was usually the case. They were removed two or three at a time, so the first one carried out brought the best chances for good trade, since the most sought-after contraband was bought or bartered right away. Items became less valuable as the day went on. A body's price would be written on a piece of paper and pinned to his clothes. Major Grigsby recalled:

> The first dozen or so would be marked as high, sometimes as [much as] three dollars apiece, and if there were eighty or a hundred in the row of corpses, as low as fifty cents

> would be [for] some of the last. If you paid three dollars for a corpse, you would get out early while trade was brisk, and before the best bargains were gone. If you paid fifty cents for a corpse you had to sit by it perhaps until after noon, and watch it to keep it from being stolen, and when it did come your turn to go, the stench of your corpse would make you sick and chances for trade would be slim.

Sometimes fights broke out over the ownership of especially valuable corpses. Grigsby even heard rumors that some of the dead were prematurely assisted on speeding their final journey just so the body would be first in line the next morning (Botkin 450-53).

In the postbellum years, the South was plagued with urban legends which all had the same general point: extreme disrespect to the remains of dead Confederates. It was bandied about in March 1866 that people who lived near the site of the Battle of Petersburg, Virginia, were unearthing skeletons of former Northern and Southern warriors and selling them to be ground into bone dust to be used as fertilizer ("The *Petersburg Index* says..." March 31, 1866 3).

The national press was outraged by stories emanating from Franklin, Tennessee, in May 1866, alleging that the burial site of hundreds of Confederates had been rented to black freedmen, who intended to plow the field and plant crops. Some panicky folk recommended emergency measures to exhume and remove the dead before they underwent such agricultural indignity ("The battlefield of Franklin, TN...." 1). Later, the location of the story changed to Virginia. Finally came a sheepish admission by journalists in September 1869: "The statement going the rounds of the press that the collection of human bones on the battlefields in Virginia, to be used as fertilizer ... is an unqualified lie" ("The statement going the rounds..." 2).

It does appear to have been true, however, that around November 1865 the skeletons of 160,000 horses and cattle killed in the Shenandoah Valley during the war were collected for processing at a bone factory near Winchester, Virginia ("There are 160,000 skeletons..." 4). Perhaps the legend got started from garbled retellings of this incident.

10
Premonitions and Prologues

A journal called *The Monthly Magazine* published a satirical article in 1821 called "Specimen of a Newspaper, A.D. 2056," which included these lines: "The army of the Northern States of America will take the field against that of the Southern Provinces early next spring. The principal Northern force will consist of 1,460,000 picked troops. General Congrove's new mechanical cannon was tried last week at the siege of Georgia. It discharged in one hour 1,120 balls, each weighing 500 pounds. The distance of the objects fired at was eleven miles, and so perfect was the engine that the whole of these balls were lodged in a space of twenty feet square" ("A Prophecy in Jest" 1).

Okay, so the writer got the year incorrect, there was no real General Congrove, no cannonball ever weighed 500 pounds (the average was 12 pounds), cannon in 1861 could not hit targets at 11 miles (the real average range was just under a mile), and the writer far underestimated the number of Northern soldiers (just under 2,130,000 total). Yet, to give the satirist some credit, he accurately predicted a war between the North and South forty years before the event. Such lucky guesses made Nostradamus's reputation.

James Buchanan, Lincoln's predecessor, isn't remembered for very much. He was the only bachelor president; his policies helped make the Civil War a certainty rather than a possibility; he was instrumental in enforcing the Guano Islands Act, passed by his precursor Franklin Pierce in 1856, a law that enabled the U.S. to seize unclaimed islands rich in that top-notch fertilizer bird guano, even allowing the president to protect the precious droppings with military force if necessary. (Guano was very much in the headlines in the 1850s. Why, the *New York Times* was full of guano—unlike now, of course!) But one thing would have made Buchanan memorable, had it come to pass. He was almost assassinated.

In early October 1858, a lunatic named W. Strong was arrested in Washington, D.C., for firing into a Freemasons' lodge. When in custody, Strong informed lawmen that he had visited the White House in December 1857 with a view to perhaps killing the president. In those pre-Secret Service days, it was only a matter of making an appointment to meet Buchanan. Strong showed up with a gun in his coat. His acid test: if Buchanan treated him kindly and with respect, Strong would graciously permit him to live. However, if the chief executive were not "kindly disposed," or maybe if he seemed distant with other things on his mind, like bird guano, Strong would shoot him. Fortunately for Buchanan, his impeccable manners impressed Strong, who left without committing mayhem. Buchanan did not realize his close shave until more than a year later ("Reported Narrow Escape of the President" 1).

What Strong was up to between December 1857 and October 1858, I have no idea.

On the night of April 12, 1865, a young inmate at the New York Institution for the Deaf and Dumb arose from her bed, awoke a fellow student, and said in sign language, "Lincoln is shot." In the morning, she could remember nothing of the incident until others told her. Her strange behavior was the subject of merely passing speculation at the school until two days later, when it became a topic of major interest. A person called "W.," presumably a member of the faculty or staff, told the story to the *New York Evening Post* on April 18 ("A Curious Incident" 1).

Of course, no one had more premonitions of Lincoln's upcoming demise than the president himself. His stories about seemingly prophetic dreams—of witnessing his own funeral in the White House, of being a passenger on an aimlessly drifting ship—have been told many times. A few such tales are not so well known.

In February 1861, before Lincoln left Springfield, Illinois, to be inaugurated, he told the members of the state's House of Representatives that he would never return and "affectionately asked that his friends would pray for and remember him." They didn't take him seriously. One member wrote an official-sounding resolution full of "whereas"-es pointing out that in Cincinnati Jesse Dubois, the Illinois Auditor of Public Accounts, and Ebenezer Peck, official reporter for the state Supreme Court, took a lock of Abe's hair to remember him by as they accompanied him on his journey to D.C. The document's mock resolution requested that Dubois and Peck give the hair to the state treasurer for safekeeping since it would be "a state treasure of inestimable value in case the president elect shall never return to the state." If and when Lincoln did return, the treasurer would be instructed to return the keepsake to him ("Legislative Joking" 1). The joke didn't seem so funny a few years later. One wonders whatever happened to the lock of hair.

Harriet Beecher Stowe visited Lincoln in January 1864. When asked about the war's progress, he told the author, "Whichever way it ends, I have the impression that I shan't last long after it is over" ("Joking and Suffering" 1.). Similarly, in July 1864, he spoke with a *Boston Journal* reporter who later recounted that even if Lincoln didn't exactly anticipate death by assassination, he had an uncanny feeling that he would come to an end at the same time as the war. During their conversation, Lincoln revealed that he was greatly troubled by anti-war sentiment in the North. When the reporter reassured him that he never doubted that right would triumph, the president replied, "Neither have I, but I may never live to see it. I feel a presentiment that I shall not outlast the rebellion. When it is over my work will be done" ("President Lincoln Had a Presentiment…" 1).

On April 9, 1865, the Sunday before Lincoln was shot, the president read aloud these lines from *Macbeth*, one of his favorite plays:

> Duncan is in his grave;
> After life's fitful fever, he sleeps well.

> Treason has done his worst: nor steel, nor poison,
> Malice domestic, foreign levy, nothing
> Can touch him further.

Lincoln's friend Isaac N. Arnold wondered, "After 'treason' had 'done his worst,' the friends who heard him on that occasion remembered that he read the passage over twice and with an absorbed and peculiar manner. Did he feel a mysterious presentiment of his approaching fate?" ("Abraham Lincoln As a Reader..." 4) On one hand, mundane events seem to take on a deeper significance after a traumatic event. On the other hand, it's still a creepy story.

A Confederate stationed at Pensacola, Florida, fell into a coma-like sleep in April 1862, so deep that his fellow soldiers gave up waking him. When he finally came out of it, he said he had had a three-part prophetic dream: He would die the next day at 4 p.m.; the greatest and bloodiest battle of the war would take place during the last week of April; and peace would be declared in early May ("A Singular Prophecy" 1).

How did the soldier's predictions pan out? The only significant action at the end of April was the Peninsular Campaign in Virginia which, while violent enough, certainly wasn't the worst of the war, and peacetime was still three years in the future. But he did fall over dead at 4 p.m. the next day.

In March 1863 another soldier, a Hawkins Zouave in New York, had a dream featuring a heavenly scroll bearing the words "Peace, April 23, 1863." A member of Captain Cabot's artillery company named Bright, stationed at Fort Warren in Boston harbor, had the very same dream four months before, which no doubt put hope in the hearts of many ("Coincidence of Dreams" 4). It was a false hope, but sometimes that is all we have.

11

Ford's Theatre: Comedy Turns to Tragedy

As we all know, on the night of April 14, 1865, President Lincoln made a seemingly trivial, yet fateful, decision: in the mood for some badly needed laughs, he went to Ford's Theatre to see the popular comedy *Our American Cousin*, produced by and starring celebrated actress Laura Keene. As an actor, John Wilkes Booth was familiar with the play and knew the biggest audience reaction came after the main character, played by Harry Hawk, uttered the line "You sockdologizing old mantrap." That was the perfect time to pull the trigger because the crowd would be most distracted. The preposterous words were the last ones Lincoln ever heard. Keene originally intended to put on a new play that fateful night, *The Workmen of Washington* ("Laura Keene has taken..." 3). Had she stuck to the plan, perhaps Lincoln would have preferred to stay home and history would have turned out differently.

In mid-May 1865—a month after *Our American Cousin* became the most notorious play in American history—Keene and her troupe were scheduled to appear at Wood's Theatre in Louisville, Kentucky. The cast included her star comedian Hawk, who had spoken that line when Booth fired the fatal shot and leapt from the Lincolns' theater box. Advertisements proclaimed that the Keene company would perform Oliver Goldsmith's 1773 play *She Stoops to Conquer* ("Wood's Theater" May 15, 1865 3), but the audience had other ideas. "By numerous requests," they wanted to see the show that had been Lincoln's last diversion.

Naturally, the *Louisville Journal* noted the calamity recently associated with the play—how could it possibly not have? "This admirable comedy was also a favorite with our late lamented President, who, on each occasion of Miss Keene's visit to Washington, attended its representation, accompanied by his family" ("Wood's Theater" May 19, 1865 3). The play went off in Louisville without a hitch, but one imagines the growing apprehension every cast member suffered, especially Hawk, as the words "You sockdologizing old mantrap" drew closer and closer. The play was so successful that Keene and Hawk performed it in the city again on October 23. "The popular demand for it is unabated," remarked the *Journal* ("Wood's Theater" October 23, 25, 1865 3).

By May 1865, Keene had staged the production more than 300 consecutive nights in New York alone and turned a personal profit of $30,000, over a half-million dollars in modern currency ("Wood's Theater" May 19, 1865 3). Nevertheless, once her audiences' morbid curiosity about the play wore off, the property proved to be more of a burden than a blessing to Keene. The public mind would never shake off its association between the actress and that tragic night. An especially bitter pill for Keene (in retrospect) was that after she bought exclusive rights to perform *Our American Cousin*, she had to fight other theatrical companies doing unauthorized productions of the play that eventually ruined her career. For example, in April 1861, almost exactly four years before Lincoln's assassination, Keene sued two Philadelphia managers who put on an illegal showing. She demanded $560 in damages and won, at least in the short run ("Damages Recovered" 1).

In December 1865, the New York Supreme Court dismissed a lawsuit she filed to stop another unauthorized production ("The suit of Miss Laura Keene..." 1). Never mind that silly "exclusive rights" concept! Her sad decline afterward is well documented in Thomas A. Bogar's book *Backstage at the Lincoln Assassination.*

12
Lincoln's Remains

After John Wilkes Booth shot Lincoln in Ford's Theatre, soldiers and civilians carried the mortally wounded president across the street to a room in Petersen's boardinghouse. Maunsel B. Field was present and eerily described the changes that overcame Lincoln after death. After a surgeon bound Lincoln's jaw closed and put silver half-dollars on his eyes to keep them from flipping open, this happened, according to Field: "The expression immediately after death was purely negative, but in fifteen minutes there came over the mouth, the nostrils, and the chin, a smile that seemed almost an effort of life. I had never seen about the President's face an expression more genial and pleasing" ("The President After Death" 3). Field opted to leave the room and the beaming-though-dead president, one imagines rather quickly.

Our death-obsessed nineteenth-century ancestors wanted every detail involving funerals and embalming and were especially eager to know how the dead appeared. If the deceased were prominent, newspaper readers' curiosity knew no bounds. Reporters were happy to oblige them in the case of America's first assassinated president. The *New York World*'s Washington correspondent described how Lincoln looked on April 20, five long days after his death. The big smile Maunsel B. Field recounted was gone and instead Lincoln now appeared firm and decisive, always admirable traits in a president. Said the reporter, "Death has fastened on his frozen face; all character and idiosyncrasy in his life has not changed one line in his countenance. The mouth is shut like that of one who had put his foot down firm, and so are the eyes which look as calm as if in slumber" ("To the Western Associated Press" April 21, 1865 3).

Lincoln's body was embalmed, placed on a train, and taken on a multi-city tour stretching from D.C. to the family crypt in Springfield, Illinois. Before the remains left the nation's capital, anyone whose home allowed a good view of the funeral procession could make a small fortune by selling a peep to the grieving. Window views could cost anywhere from $10 to $25, roughly $170 and $422 respectively in modern currency. One newsboy sold his place in the top of a tree for 25 cents, now equal to slightly under $5 ("Good places for seeing the procession…" 1). As is well known, thousands of mourners gazed upon Lincoln at every stop. The part history books don't tell: the undertaker's preservation was temporary at best, so on the trip Lincoln had to be re-embalmed sporadically.

Sketch of Lincoln lying in state in New York City Hall, April 24–25, 1865. (*Library of Congress Prints and Photographs Division*)

For example, a reporter who saw the body on April 24 wrote, "The embalmers ... rearranged the body, which had been somewhat disturbed by the journey, after which the lid was removed, affording a view of the face and upper part of the breast.... The appearance of the dead President bears no marks of pain, but the eyes are sunk, and the face is somewhat discolored and sallow about the lower part; dark around the eyes and cheeks, and lips very lightly compressed" ("Business in the city..." 3).

A reporter writing from New York on April 25 stated, "The appearance of the body indicated that the embalming had not been perfect. The discoloration is daily increasing, and it is thought the coffin cannot be opened after leaving the city" ("To the Western Associated Press" April 26, 1865 3). Clearly, it was time to give Lincoln a touch-up.

On May 3, the day Lincoln arrived home in Illinois, he looked worse yet. "The face of Mr. Lincoln does not wear a natural hue," wrote the *Louisville Journal*'s Springfield correspondent. "The sunken eyes, the sharp features, and the dark color about the brow and temples, do not make the President seem what he was in life." (In other words, the embalmers' heroic efforts to thwart nature were failing.) "There is no expression here; the generous smile and beaming light seem to have departed with the flight of his immortal soul to the realms of a purer land" ("Our Springfield Correspondence" 1). That was a diplomatic way of saying his facial expression seemed "unnatural"—exactly the word his widow, Mary Todd Lincoln, used to describe it, and the reason she refused to allow the body to be photographed.

"The coffin will be closed at nine o'clock tomorrow [May 4], and the public are gazing upon the face of the dead for the last time," wrote the *Journal*'s man ("Our Springfield Correspondence" 1). But he was wrong. Lincoln's body was exposed to the daylight several times more: on December 21, 1865, September 19, 1871, October 9, 1874, and April 14, 1887. And that's not even counting the time a gang of body snatchers almost made off with him in November 1876. To prevent further attempted theft, he was exhumed on September 26, 1901, and reburied in a steel cage encased in concrete, never to be seen by mortal eye again.

Since we are on the topic of our ancestors' longing to know details about the appearance of the celebrated (and the commonplace) dead, let's examine the only postmortem appearance of Illinois Senator Stephen A. Douglas, Lincoln's chief political rival. Douglas's coffin was opened in June 1868 to move his remains to an ornate mausoleum in Chicago. The Little Giant was in such fine condition that he looked for all the world as though he were ready to hop out of his casket and debate Lincoln once again. Reporters probably would rather have died themselves than disappoint readers who wanted precise details. "Upon removing the lid covering the glass, the face of the illustrious Senator was found to be in a remarkable state of preservation, almost as natural as when buried seven years ago, excepting that the eyes are more sunken, the nose more contracted, and the surface of the forehead somewhat indented or pitted."

On the plus side, "the complexion is very fair, the contour of the head and face apparently unchanged, and the expression quite natural and plainly recognizable. The hair looks as glossy and black as ever, and the raiment appears as neat and tidy as when first put on, not presenting the least evidence of mildew or discoloration" ("Senator Douglas" 3). All of this was considered very good to know.

Above: Lincoln's body is removed from his Springfield tomb, 1901. (*Library of Congress Prints and Photographs Division*)

Left: Stephen A. Douglas. He looked just great after burial! (*Library of Congress Prints and Photographs Division*)

13

Quack the Ripper

Francis Tumblety was the last child born into a large Irish family in 1833, not long before the entire clan moved to Rochester, New York. FBI profilers John Douglas and Mark Olshaker relate that the industrious but already unsavory teenage Tumblety sold pornography for a few extra coppers, then in adulthood made a very good living as an itinerant homeopathist and "herb doctor"—that is to say, a quack and patent medicine peddler. While his home base was St. Louis, he traveled the nation selling his suspect wares and getting into a variety of legal scrapes (Douglas and Olshaker 75). He also cultivated a moustache so wide that it looks like one could do chin-ups on it.

Washington, D.C., was one city in Tumblety's orbit in the mid-1860s. He donned military uniforms that he was not legally entitled to wear and claimed to be on a first-name basis with the president and General Grant (Douglas and Olshaker 75). Almost certainly he wasn't, but he did know David Herold, described by a reporter as Tumblety's "agent and confidante" ("A boy has been arrested..." 3). Herold also was a confidante of John Wilkes Booth. After Lincoln's assassination and Booth's escape, the authorities wanted to interview anyone who knew Booth or his inner circle. The police reasoned that if the herb doctor was acquainted with Herold in D.C., it wasn't such a stretch to think that he might know Booth too and been privy to his plans. The hunt for Tumblety was on! His national reputation for sleaziness was already such by May 1865 that a reporter writing about the search for the so-called doctor described him as "notorious" ("A boy has been arrested..." 3).

Tumblety, using the pseudonym "J.H. Blackburn," was arrested in St. Louis on May 5 and brought to Washington ("J.H. Blackburn..." 1; "Tumblety, alias Blackburn..." 1). He was clapped into the Old Capitol prison, the same jail that was home at various times to Confederate spy Belle Boyd; Southern army cavalry battalion commander John Mosby; Henry Wirz, operator of the Confederate prison at Andersonville; and other suspected assassination plotters, including Dr. Mudd, Mary Surratt, and theater owner John T. Ford. Unlike some of these persons, Tumblety wasn't tried, hanged, or even called as a trial witness, so it appears the government felt he had no connection to the conspiracy—and this was at a time when Secretary of War Edwin Stanton and army investigator Lafayette C. Baker were seemingly arresting and jailing everyone who

Francis Tumblety: medical quack, weirdo, and friend of Lincoln conspirator David Herold. Also Jack the Ripper? (*Wikimedia*)

ever so much as gave Lincoln a dirty look. Tumblety's friend Herold was hanged in the nation's capital along with three other accused conspirators on July 7, 1865.

Tumblety was free to continue vending his nostrums and staying a step ahead of the law, but here is where his story takes a very interesting turn indeed. He was in London, England, in the summer and autumn of 1888. His decidedly strange behavior there made him a Jack the Ripper suspect. He made British stiff upper lips pucker a little when he made it known to various medical schools that he would purchase the inner sexual organs of female cadavers (Sugden xxv). He explained that he planned to write a learned treatise on that topic and include a genuine specimen with each copy sold! In fact, Tumblety did amass a collection of preserved female reproductive organs and had these prized keepsakes at the time of his death (Douglas and Olshaker 76).

A bizarre fellow to be sure, but was he the Ripper? In recent years there has been a push to make Tumblety a leading suspect. It does appear that some British detectives had suspicions even at the time. They knew that the Ripper had removed and carried away the sex organs from two victims, so you can see how some arrived at that conclusion. The arguments usually boil down to the fact that he held women in contempt; that he expressed unhealthy anatomical interests; that he was in London at the right time; that the Ripper murders ceased after he left Britain in mid-November 1888; and that the famous red ink "Dear Boss" letter the Ripper allegedly sent to the press included American phrases. However, the last bit of evidence is especially shaky, as most Ripper experts agree that the "Dear Boss" letter was a journalist's forgery (Douglas and Olshaker 45-53; Sugden 270-73).

An additional plank of the theory is that the Ripper's victims were mutilated with what some consider "surgical skill," and Tumblety was a doctor. However, Jack's degree of medical expertise is highly debatable, and even if he did have such skills, it must be remembered that Tumblety was not a real doctor. He was an impudent quack, not an accomplished surgeon.

Apart from psychological and behavioral objections to the theory—for example, Tumblety was never known to have exhibited such dangerous pathology against women either before or after the Ripper murders, and a killer as far gone mentally as the Ripper was not going to just grow a conscience and stop—there are a couple of serious problems. One is that Tumblety's taste ran to homosexual rape, not strangling and disemboweling middle-aged female prostitutes. British police arrested Tumblety on November 16, 1888, for "gross indecency" and indecently assaulting at least four men, charges dating back to July (Douglas and Olshaker 75-76; Sugden xxv). The other obstacle is that Tumblety was in his mid-fifties in 1888, which would make him rather old to be the Ripper. Not impossible, but very unlikely.

Tumblety fled England before his trial and went back to the USA under another pseudonym, Frank Townsend. He died in St. Louis in 1903. If Tumblety were Jack the Ripper—he wasn't, but if he were—one could plausibly claim that at least one person who colluded to kill Lincoln, David Herold, had ties to the most famous serial killer of all time. Here is a chance for Ripperologists and Lincoln assassination conspiracy theorists to combine everything into one overarching master plot.

14

Mrs. Surratt and Other Post-Assassination Events

One unpleasant facet of human nature, among so many, is the urge to collect morbid souvenirs at scenes of notorious murders or executions. Most of us deny this impulse, possibly out of sheer embarrassment, but it seems that our nineteenth-century predecessors were more up front about it. Take what happened to alleged Lincoln assassination conspirator Mary Surratt, for example.

As students of American history know, those arrested for the assassination included Dr. Samuel Mudd, David Herold, Lewis Powell (aka Payne), George Atzerodt, Michael O'Laughlen, Samuel Arnold, and Mrs. Surratt. Another suspect, her son John Surratt, escaped the law—at least, for a while. The government argued with dubious logic that since Mrs. Surratt owned the D.C. boardinghouse where the plot was hatched, she must have been in on it as well.

The conspirators' trial provoked controversy that lasts to this day concerning whether it was legal and proper to hold a military trial for civilians, and whether Mrs. Surratt was innocent since the evidence against her was weak at best. Her chief accuser, her boarder Louis Weichmann, later admitted—after it was far too late to help her—that his testimony had been coerced and a lie ("The Trial and Execution" 1; Bogar 249-50). Mudd, O'Laughlen, and Arnold were sentenced to life in prison; Herold, Powell, and Atzerodt were sentenced to die. So was Mrs. Surratt, much to the surprise of those who thought the government would not execute a woman, especially on such paltry evidence. But hanged she was, along with the other three, on July 7, 1865. Among her last words, directed at Lieutenant Colonel W. H. H. McCall, who was duty-bound to handcuff her, lead her to the gallows, and support her until the trapdoor opened: "You are a scoundrel!" ("The duty of placing…" 1). Mrs. Surratt's boardinghouse still exists and is said to be haunted by her understandably peeved spirit.

But to return to the subject of death souvenirs. It was reported a week after the hanging that relic hunters had cut the portico in front of her boardinghouse to splinters. One ghoul offered a servant $100 (today, equal to almost $1,700) for any piece of Mrs. Surratt's clothing, and someone unsuccessfully offered the same amount for an inch of the hanging rope ("The Trial and Execution" 1; "One hundred dollars were offered..." 3). Mrs. Surratt's worldly possessions were sold at auction in mid-October ("The effects of the late..." 1).

In a similar story, a room at the Merchants' Hotel in Montreal where conspirator Lewis Powell stayed became a lucrative tourist attraction. The landlord kept it in the same condition as Powell left it ("The room occupied..." 1).

Where was former Republican Senator Preston King, currently the Collector of New York City's Custom House? He had been making himself so scarce for days that rumor held he resigned his post or had done something more drastic. The signs were not encouraging. For a week, starting on November 7, 1865, he had been "laboring under an attack of nervous disability," as the press said ("To the Associated Press" 3). That is, King had a nervous breakdown. On November 13, he left his room at the Astor House Hotel, saying only that he was going for a walk, and disappeared. Ominously, he purchased a 25-pound bag of bullets on this final stroll ("It has been ascertained..." 3). The next day, two children said they saw him jump off a Hoboken ferryboat with that shot bag tied around his neck. His body was not recovered, but a hat was, and prominent politician Thurlow Weed recognized it as King's ("To the Associated Press" 3).

For days, the river teemed with boats and searchers with grappling hooks, but no one collected King or the $500 reward for his body ("A reward of $500..." 3). The search was called off on November 29 ("The Custom House authorities..." 3), leading to another rumor alleging that King wasn't dead after all—that he was in hiding to regain his health and would reemerge when he saw fit ("A rumor comes..." 1). The rumor was scotched permanently on May 14, 1866, when his corpse surfaced in the Atlantic basin at Brooklyn. "The remains ... are not much bloated and are less decomposed than might have been expected," a wire service said hopefully. Their positive spin was contradicted in the very same report, which also asserted that "the face was so much disfigured ... as to be hardly recognizable" ("The remains of Preston King..." 3; "Preston King's Body Recovered" 1.). Nevertheless, King's nephew identified him, as did a Custom House official ("Officer Kenny..." 3). He was buried in Ogdensburg.

But what has King to do with Mary Surratt, you may be asking? The official reason for King's suicide was that he was depressed by his inability to clean up corruption at the Custom House ("It is said the rascalities..." 3; "The unfortunate death..." 1), but what may have been the real reason leaked in July 1867. A newspaper reported that he was tormented by remorse for not allowing Surratt's daughter to meet with President Johnson to plead for her mother's life. "This is no new story; neither is it without foundation, and pretty strong foundation," argued the *Philadelphia Daily News*. "The mother was executed—*murdered*.... [A]ll this proved too much for a man naturally as kind-hearted as was Preston King" ("Preston King and Mrs. Surratt" 4).

Then there are little-known but interesting circumstances involving possible, untried conspirators. Considering that Lincoln was announced to be attending Ford's Theatre that fatal Friday night—and it was rumored General Grant would be there too—why were the building's upper rows of seats entirely empty when one would expect a packed house? An unknown person or persons rented all the private boxes at Ford's on the morning of the event, except for the one occupied by the Lincolns and their guests. Whoever paid for the seats never turned up, suggesting that someone wanted the boxes empty and free from possibly interfering witnesses ("A New Proof of the Premeditation" 3).

New York Senator Preston King. It seems likely that guilt over Mary Surratt's prosecution drove him to his grave. (*Library of Congress Prints and Photographs Division*)

George B. Love, a fired hospital steward, was arrested on April 19 after he tried to dodge military pickets surrounding D.C. at several locations, indicating perhaps that he badly wanted to escape the city. The press described Love as "about five feet ten inches high, light curly high and beard, small feet, delicate hands, and ... evidently educated. He had on a new fine officers' fatigue coat, gray pants and vest, new underclothing, double and fine calf boots." He was taken to the guard room at Fort Thayer but soldiers did not examine him closely enough. There he took a hidden penknife and cut the jugular vein on each side of his neck. "It is thought that he knew something of the late assassination," the press mused darkly ("On Wednesday night..." 1; "The name..." 1). Could Love have been a conspirator who got away?

Consider also a tantalizing news item dated April 28, 1865:

> A well known citizen of Baltimore committed suicide last Monday a short distance from this city, by shooting himself with a pistol. No cause could be assigned for the deed, except that he had recently seemed depressed and melancholy. Subsequent events have induced the suspicion that he was in some way implicated in the conspiracy, and last night the body was exhumed, embalmed, and sent to Washington by order of the government. The affair causes much speculation, and there are many reports in connection with it, some of the facts of which it is deemed imprudent to publish at present. ("A well known citizen" 3)

That's the last we hear of it, imprudent facts and all, but the government's investigators must have taken the anonymous Baltimorean seriously as a conspiracy suspect since they wanted his body shipped to them.

15

Belated Explosives

Thousands of cannonballs, torpedoes, and mortars were fired during the war. Many did what they were invented to do, while others were lost in forests, lakes, fields, or other terrain. Not all of this weaponry could be accounted for, and some waited patiently to do their job—for months, for years, even for decades.

A torpedo sunk in Charleston harbor, South Carolina, *circa* 1863, was forgotten but remembered when it suddenly went off in June 1866, dousing interested spectators with geysers of water ("A torpedo..." 1.). Another one went off in Charleston two months later, this time destroying a ship and a bystander ("A forgotten torpedo..." 4).

Also in June 1866, a young boy hunting near Atlanta, Georgia, was disappointed when he ran out of ammunition. Fortunately (or so he thought), an unexploded shell from the late war lay nearby. He tried to get gunpowder out of it. His obituary said, "Result: shell exploded, and no boy to be found" ("A Negro boy..." 1).

On January 24, 1867, several cartridges from the last days of the Confederacy went off in a comically inappropriate location: a crockery store in Montgomery, Alabama. Amazingly, no damage was done except to the nerves of the establishment's occupants ("An explosion took place..." 2).

In January or February 1867, three Charleston men engaged in the fascinating but nerve-wracking task of drawing powder out of an unexploded shell. The tally was one dead, two wounded, and lots of broken glass in the vicinity ("Three Charleston..." 2).

In December 1868, Hiram Reeves of Port Gibson, Mississippi, was nearly killed when an unexploded Parrott shell in his house transformed into an exploded one. Reeves had been using it unwisely as an andiron—that is, a metal brace that holds wood in a fireplace ("Hiram Reeves..." 2).

During the war, Profit Island, located 4 miles below Port Hudson, Louisiana, was a repository for explosive devices colloquially called "lamp-posts." On July 22, 1870, a group of men and boys wondered about a missile's inner workings and satisfied their idle curiosity by dismantling it—with a steel hatchet and a chisel. The 150-pound shell went off, killing instantly two men, two boys, and wounding one youth. Those killed became "an indistinguishable mass of human flesh," said a report ("A dreadful incident..." 2).

Rumor held that a can of nitroglycerine was buried somewhere in Raleigh, North Carolina's Capitol Square just before Lee's surrender. But no one could remember its exact location, and as late as November 1873 townspeople expressed understandable reluctance to do any digging or development in the area ("There is said to be..." 1).

The blade at Parker's Sawmill in Milan, Tennessee, struck something hard on January 5, 1892, sending pieces of broken saw flying everywhere and badly injuring William Berry. The object turned out to be a small cannonball left in the trunk by Nathan Bedford Forrest ("A Cannon Ball in a Tree" 7).

During the Civil War, Confederates ditched a number of bombs and ammo into Buffalo Bayou in Houston, Texas, so they could not be seized by Union forces. On March 31, 1892, a boy named Charlie Harris pulled one of the old bombs out of the water and took it home, presumably to see if it still had any explosive power. When he struck it with an ax, he found that the rebels' bomb-making skills were quite up to par ("Success with a Vengeance" 2).

Mr. Bailey of Crawford, Laurel County, Kentucky, was plowing one day in March 1907 when he unearthed a very old cap-and-ball pistol from the Civil War era. Its wooden handle had long since rotted off and the barrel was rusted, so Mr. Bailey tossed the relic away as being useless. But Bailey's ten-year-old son Leander and his cousin Sidney Bailey, age eight, were smitten with the old weapon. They retrieved it, examined it, played with it. Little Sidney pounded the seemingly harmless old relic with a rock. But it still contained a brass percussion cap and the gunpowder within had been protected from the elements. The gun went off, discharging a bullet into Leander Bailey's abdomen and killing him instantly ("Pistol Long Buried..." 1).

Ernest Patterson was hunting near his home in Dundee, Kentucky, in January 1911, when he found an interesting relic of the late war: an unexploded shell. He took it home and tried to see what made it tick, so to speak, by prying it open with a hatchet. Soon thereafter, Ernest had three fingers fewer ("Old War Shells Are Dangerous" 4).

During the war, Jackson Riggins of New Providence (now part of Clarksville), Tennessee, buried an unexploded shell. It remained out of harm's way for half a century until 1916, when he unearthed it and brought it home very carefully. The Riggins's daughter, Mrs. A. E. Edmondson, made headlines on March 22, 1917, when she put the shell in her car and drove to town with it. Today such an event would call for the evacuation of entire city blocks and a visit from the bomb squad; back then, the bemused press noted that the family considered the shell "a valued heirloom" ("Bombshell, Relic of Civil War..." 9).

Mike Rogers was plowing his farm near the Dix River in Garrard County, Kentucky, in May 1922, when he dug up a pristine cannonball which, fortunately for Rogers, remained in that condition. Most likely, it had been lost during the retreat from Perryville ("Cannon Ball Found" 6).

Then there is the relatively recent cautionary tale of Sam W., a Chester, Virginia, Civil War relic collector who died in February 2008 when a 140-year-old, 75-pound naval shell he was restoring exploded despite his having successfully disarmed 1,600 other shells. One piece of shrapnel landed on the porch of a house a quarter mile away (Mustermann).

How many lost, potentially unstable Civil War explosive devices remain out there? "Tons," say experts (Mustermann).

Felix Zollicoffer, brigadier general in the CSA and postmortem poet. (*Library of Congress Prints and Photographs Division*)

16

Things They Left Behind

The soldiers' (and sometimes civilians') legacies include postmortem poetry, faithful dogs, a defaced battlefield building, a disembodied voice, hardtack biscuits, farm chores, their own skeletons, petrified bodies, abandoned limbs, human remains in government files, sealed personal effects, a vengeful ghost, buried treasure, antique bloodstains, curious epitaphs, defiantly long hair, and a secret tunnel.

After Confederate General Felix Zollicoffer died in battle on January 19, 1862, his ghost composed a poem about his own death—speaking in the third person, at that—and transmitted it to medium Lucretia Russell. That's what she said, anyway. Here are a few sample verses, the contemplation of which may make the reader wish he/she also were dead:

He lay upon the battlefield,
His lips gave not a sound,
He fought with brave and manly aid
When on the battle ground.

Brave Zollicoffer called his men,
I'm dying, men, cried he,
And from this day forever more
I never shall happy be.

Another General gave command,
I could not hear that sound.
But off they ran and left me there
Dead—lifeless on the ground. ("On the Death of Zollicoffer" 3)

Not to be outdone, a Spiritualist newspaper published in August 1866 some recent verses by none other than the fourteen-months-dead John Wilkes Booth, whose current address was in "the seventh sphere." Touchingly, Booth's ghost regretted an unnamed rash action of his, perhaps something involving a theater, as his poem began "Oh, God! what fiery waves of hell across my burdened conscience roll!" It ended with this literally deathless couplet: "Ye hoary age, ye thoughtless youth, / Avoid the fate of John Wilkes Booth!" ("A Spiritualistic paper…" 1).

Lieutenant Pfieff of Illinois brought his dog along on his campaigns. After Pfieff fell at Shiloh, the pet sat by his grave and refused to move for twelve days, except for taking brief meals. The dog ceased the vigil only when he saw Pfieff's widow approaching in search of the grave and got up to lead her right to the spot ("A Faithful Dog" 1).

Concerning a similar tale from West Virginia, the *Louisville Journal* expressed healthy skepticism. "The story has a fishy odor," it said, "but the *Wheeling Intelligencer* says it is vouched for by respectable authority." A soldier from the 106th New York Infantry died at New Creek in Mineral County in 1865. A dog he had adopted was found lying inconsolable on the grave. There he stayed for three years, except for an occasional lunch break. In 1868 the soldiers buried in the cemetery were exhumed and moved for reburial at the military cemetery in Grafton. The dog fled for the woods as the workmen dug and wasn't seen for days, but then he turned up at his master's new grave, all settled in for more hopeful, hopeless waiting ("A Fish Story" 4).

Maryland's Battle of Antietam took place on September 17, 1862, and ended with 23,000 soldiers dead, wounded, or missing. Nearly a year later, in July 1863, a war correspondent noted that the location of "the bloodiest day in American history" showed little sign of the horrors enacted there. The place resembled a bucolic paradise with "golden wheat, scented clover, and luxuriant corn." Only a few trees bore scars of battle. But there was one discordant note against the harmony: a small building, either a schoolhouse or a church, was pockmarked with cannonball holes and obscene graffiti written on the inner walls by soldiers from both sides ("The Field of Antietam" 1).

The mother of Decatur M. Boyden of the 7th Rhode Island was climbing the cellar stairs in Woonsocket on that day in 1864 when she clearly heard her son saying "Oh, mother!" The voice was so close she thought he must have somehow come home, but

Above: Joseph D. Mitchell's hardtack tombstone. (*Photo courtesy of Stacy Barnes, City Administrator of Greensburg, KS*)

Left: Close-up showing the hardtack biscuit in the window. (*Photo courtesy of Stacy Barnes*)

there was no Decatur M. Boyden to be found. She became convinced that her son must have been killed or wounded. She didn't tell anyone about the experience, yet that night two family members who lived apart from Mrs. Boyden dreamed that Decatur had been wounded. Later the family discovered that on the day Mrs. Boyden heard the voice, Decatur had in fact been wounded in the side in Virginia—though not fatally since he died in 1913 ("Singular Circumstances" 1).

T. F. Perkins of Hartsville, Tennessee, served in Pickett's Division, 11th Virginia Cavalry. When he attended a Confederate veterans' reunion in Birmingham in June 1916, he brought a strange keepsake, a hardtack biscuit that was among the last rations served at Gettysburg. A reporter describing the dubious morsel, which had endured a half-century, said it was "hard as a brick." But, Perkins added, "It always was" ("Keeps 'Hardtack'" 3).

Another veteran, Joseph D. Mitchell of Greensburg, Kansas, who died in 1916, was proud of his service. His grave marker informs that he had been a sergeant in Co. A, 123rd Illinois Volunteers, part of Wilder's Brigade Mounted Infantry (the celebrated "Lightning Brigade"). However, his tombstone includes an endearingly eccentric touch. In a glass window in the upper right corner, the spectator can see a genuine Civil War hardtack biscuit, looking distinctly unappetizing, that Mitchell must have had left over at the end of the conflict (Barnes). Mitchell's granite monument—which ironically kind of resembles a gigantic biscuit from a distance, if you squint—and the cracker within even survived a 2007 tornado that destroyed 95 percent of the town.

William K. Gates of Lee, Massachusetts, sent his son Charles to drive the cows to pasture one day in 1861. Charles went on his way, complete with his lunch. But he didn't come home. Not a trace of him could be found, and his parents gave up searching—until he suddenly reappeared in 1864, right at chore time and ready to finish herding the livestock as commanded, just as if he hadn't been gone a single hour. Where had he been all this time? Off to secretly join the 10th Massachusetts Regiment, which his father had forbidden in 1861, as he was underage ("Amusing Incident" 1).

People minding their own business just kept finding combatants' remains in unexpected (and expected) places. Not surprisingly, many were found in the days soon after the war ended, but some were discovered long after. In April 1866, for example, the folks in Wadesboro, North Carolina, were perturbed when they found a long-forgotten skeleton at rest under a tree, complete with gray uniform and red artillery braid ("Near Wadesboro..." 3).

In May 1866, a passerby found a skeleton near William McDaniel's house, 4 miles from Moulton, Alabama. The area had seen a battle between Generals Phillip Roddey (South) and Eli Long (North) on May 29, 1864, so the body probably had been there two years. The remains told a sad, silent tale. The uniform was Confederate, and a tintype of a woman and child was among the skeleton's possessions. Its jawbone had been broken by a musket bullet. Most likely, the wounded soldier had wandered away from the battlefield, died under the tree, been written off as a deserter, and forgotten ("The Remains of a Confederate Soldier" 4).

A laborer digging near Mobile, Alabama, in August 1866 unearthed a double surprise: a deceased Union soldier no one knew anything about, and as a bonus the body had petrified. "There are many *bold* Federal soldiers living," punned a newspaper account, "but this is a *boulder*" ("The *Mobile Advertiser* says..." 3). Another petrified body, this

THE BATTLE OF THE PETERSBURG CRATER. 555

THE CRATER, AS SEEN FROM THE UNION SIDE. FROM A SKETCH MADE AT THE TIME.

In October, 1887, Major James C. Coit, of Cheraw, South Carolina, wrote as follows with regard to this picture, and the Confederate battery, under his command, bear- on the day of the explosion. This battery [Wright's], where I was during the engagement, was just across the ravine to our left of the crater and just in rear of our infantry line, about

Havoc wrought at the Battle of the Crater. (*Library of Congress Prints and Photographs Division*)

one a captain and once a "very large, fine-looking man," was uncovered where it lay on a sand bar in Vicksburg, Mississippi, in April 1867. Said a marveling reporter, "Not only were the face, hair, whiskers, etc., perfectly natural, but every part of the uniform, though one mass of stone, was perfect" ("New Military Cemetery at Vicksburg" 3). The fossilized warrior weighed so much that he nearly sank the boat employed in bringing him ashore. Most probable explanation: the "petrification" was simply adiopocere.

About a decade after the war began, someone found a unique keepsake near a Missouri battlefield: a soldier's petrified hand and forearm, "showing every wrinkle of the flesh, the nails on the fingers, and the joints." Undoubtedly this relic had been amputated by a surgeon and then lost until rediscovered. In June 1871, the relic was reportedly on display in a Detroit drugstore ("A Detroit druggist…" 3).

Speaking of amputated limbs, the North used Dr. Wallace's office in Fredericksburg, Virginia, as a makeshift hospital. As was customary, surgeons sliced off arms and legs and then tossed the mangled parts out the window. The limbs generally were buried, but in this case, they were somehow forgotten until July 1871, when the mound unpleasant to contemplate was rediscovered ("The *Fredericksburg* [VA] *News* says..." 2).

The Battle of the Crater was a prime example of creative wartime mayhem. The opposing sides had reached a stalemate at Petersburg, Virginia, so little action was going on—on the surface, that is. Under the earth was a different story. Union General Burnside's men were slowly, quietly, digging a tunnel under the Southern lines. The plan was to pack the mine with explosives and blow the rebels skyward. The laborious plot came to fruition on July 30, 1864. When the powder was touched off, the Northerners had the element of surprise in their favor—at first! The seemingly surefire Union victory became a win for the Confederates when the Federals rode into the immense crater, making them sitting ducks for sharpshooters with a superior vantage point. Soon after this defeat, the usually patient Lincoln gave Burnside his walking papers. And there was another grim result. The ground surrounding the crater was so rich with fragmented Confederate bones that in April 1866 the landowner said it was impossible to farm it without disturbing the dead. A Richmond, Virginia, newspaper suggested that the area be turned into an official cemetery ("It is suggested by a Richmond paper..." 3).

Lieutenant Edwin Reade of the 3rd Ohio Regiment was held as a prisoner of war along with General Truman Seymour in a house on Broad Street in Charleston, South Carolina. After Reade escaped in 1864, slaves smuggled him into a house on Legare Street. Reade died in hiding, leaving the slaves in a predicament that can only be imagined. They decided to wrap him in a coarse cloth—since there was no coffin to be had and no one dared seek one—bury him in the cellar, and keep quiet. But somebody spilled the beans, and on February 27, 1867, an extraordinarily well-preserved Reade was exhumed. The members of local black churches knew of at least six other Union soldiers who had been secretly buried in the city, and now that it was safe to talk—they did ("The Charleston..." 3).

On April 16, 1880, Richard White, a farmer who lived 3 miles from Richmond, Virginia, plowed up an enormous object that was neither edible nor welcome: a skeleton, identifiable as a soldier's by the military buttons the earth yielded with it. The dead man was assumed to have been killed at a nearby battle in August 1862. Whoever he was, he must have been a giant in life. His skull measured 24 inches in circumference ("Richmond *Herald*" 2).

In April 1891, fifty skeletons were unearthed in a mass grave near Corpus Christi, Texas. Nobody knew who they were, but former soldier William Payne of Whitewright had a theory. He recalled that near the end of the war, dozens of soldiers in his unit deserted in Hunt County and headed for Mexico. None was ever seen or heard from again, and Payne thought they had all been arrested and executed ("A Bony Mystery Revealed" 1).

Laborers in Henderson, Tennessee, rang in New Year 1892 with a unique adventure. On January 2, they watched the chimney of a house they were constructing shoot down into the ground as though it were descending in an elevator, taking a portion of the house with it. There was a small, previously unknown, cave under the building site. And in the cave lay bits of four skeletons, one of which wore blue tatters and the visor of a Union soldier's cap. A rotten leather case contained a letter to Miss Wena (Rowena, one presumes) Lanty of Connersville, Indiana. The author's signature was illegible. The townsfolk put the skeleton on display so all might gape and wonder ("A Soldier's Skeleton" 5).

On August 24, 1901, workers leveling a plat of ground at a brickyard near Richmond, Kentucky, found a skeleton. The mystery was short-lived. G. B. Turley instantly knew it was an unknown Confederate he had helped bury after the Battle of Richmond. Turley identified him by his distinctive hat, which was in a perfect state of preservation ("Skeleton of Unknown Confederate Soldier" 5).

John Hardin of Persimmon, Monroe County, Kentucky, was removing dirt from a cave on his property on April 15, 1907. He intended to use it as fertilizer for his garden. Two feet below the surface he found a skeleton, well preserved by the cave's saltpeter. No one knew his identity, but probably he was a victim of one of the many guerrilla bands that had roamed the area ("Digs Up Skeleton of Human Being" 1).

In contrast to this unknown body, in a similar case not long afterward the dead was identified by someone with an excellent memory. On September 2, 1909, workers on L. C. Price's farm grading a road from Lexington to Nicholasville, Kentucky, unearthed a terra cotta casket—baked clay, that is, a favored material for flowerpots and about the last thing you'd expect a coffin to be made of. When it was opened, onlookers saw the skeleton of a very small young man clad in shreds of gray cloth and rusty brass buttons, one of which bore the letter "I" for infantry. His leather shoes were in good condition. Old-timers remembered that fifty years before, an undertaker named J. W. Patterson had specialized in terra cotta coffins. It seemed that the skeleton's identity would remain a mystery since he had no means of identification, but Chicago resident Mrs. Thomas Montague related that her husband had owned the property during the war and that in 1862 she had tended to a wounded Confederate named Lawson, a member of General Kirby Smith's army. After he died, he was buried in the spot where the skeleton was found nearly a half-century later. Lawson was buried among his comrades in Lexington Cemetery in October ("Terra Cotta Coffin Unearthed" 5; "Partially Identify Body of Confederate" 8).

In August 1866, a young boy explored the warehouse on the corner of Wapping and St. Clair Streets in Frankfort, Kentucky, a building that had been the Quartermaster's Department in the recent war. A coffee sack caught his attention. One imagines that when he looked in, he had the immortal soul scared out of him when the mummified severed head of a black woman stared back at him. The authorities hadn't the slightest idea who she was or how her head came to be considered government property ("'Dead Head' Extraordinary" 1).

Later in the same month a similar incident occurred during the clearing of the quartermaster's storehouse on East Bay Street in Charleston, South Carolina. Two boxes contained Private H. J. Hall, Company B, 3rd New Hampshire Volunteers, and Private Albert S. Flint, Company C, 4th New Hampshire Volunteers. Hall died on July 18, 1863, and Flint on August 8, 1863 ("A Strange Discovery" 1). Why had they been boxed up, stored, and overlooked as if they had been surplus government beef, no one could or would say.

A package containing a soldier's property was placed in a vault in Little Rock, Arkansas, in 1865 and then forgotten until it was rediscovered in 1883. It included a letter addressed to his friends, which was finally delivered to his family, who had moved out of the state and spent eighteen years wondering what happened to him ("A package which..." 7).

Mr. Mangrum killed a man during the war. Perhaps this preyed on his conscience. The mode of his own death suggests it did. When deer hunting north of Corinth, Mississippi, in July 1868, Mangrum saw a sheet-clad figure approaching him in the forest. Mangrum ordered it to cease. It did not. Mangrum emptied the contents of two guns into it. It continued, undaunted and determined. Mangrum climbed a tree in terror and later told friends that it stood at the base and stared up at him. He also said he recognized it as the shade of the man he had slain in battle. Mangrum fell unconscious out of the tree. He died at home a couple of days later "in great agony," raving that the entity had followed him even there. Whether it was an authentic spirit or a hallucination sired by his guilty feelings made no difference to Mangrum in the end ("Ghost or Goblin" 1).

John Scott, a veteran writing from Murfreesboro, North Carolina, told this tale in 1871: fellow soldier Nathan Beale was killed during the Seven Days' Battles at Richmond, Virginia, in 1862. Scott saw Beale's body, complete with death wound, buried three days later. In 1868, Scott stood at the Franklin depot with W. K. Ralls, S. E. Beale (the dead man's cousin), and A. M. Gardiner of Southampton County, Virginia. The four men saw a very familiar and long-gone, figure approach. Scott asked, "Is this not Nathan Beale?"

The apparition responded, "It is."

"Where have you been?"

"I am dead."

"Where are you going?"

"That is for me to know."

The secretive ghost trudged away, leaving behind four badly frightened men. Scott said he was willing to swear to the truth of his story ("Two Ghost Stories" 2).

The Confederacy often tried to draft John Duncan of Loudon County, Tennessee—so often, in fact, that he finally became an implacable foe of the Lost Cause. He attained a reputation as a bushwhacker. On one occasion Duncan was seen near Sweetwater, a town in Monroe and McMinn Counties, riding behind a captured Confederate cavalry lieutenant whom he had covered with a rifle. The two rode into the woods. An hour later Duncan came out alone, riding his own horse and leading the lieutenant's steed. The officer was never seen again, and the inference was that Duncan had murdered and buried him somewhere in the trackless forest.

The area was later purchased by John Sherold. When his son got married, Sherold granted him permission to build a house nearby. In the spring of 1892, the younger Sherold was clearing land when he uncovered a grave containing a skeleton, plus several buttons and a belt, all marked CSA. Other relics in the grave indicted that the occupant was a Confederate cavalry officer. Apparently, John Duncan's private graveyard had been found. The remains were respectfully buried under a mound.

But this was not good enough for the restless dead. The newlywed Sherold and his wife were relaxing by the stove one night when the shadowy form of a Confederate cavalry officer entered their house with as much cheek as though he owned the place. He stood around for an estimated five minutes, giving the couple a good chance to behold his presence, and then slowly dissolved into the air.

Over the next six months the form repeated this performance twenty times. On one occasion he gave the Sherolds an extra treat: They heard a gunshot coming from the vicinity of the grave, followed by a sound not unlike that of a body plopping onto the ground. Word got out, and neighbors insisted on seeing the ghost for themselves. Dozens of residents of Loudon, Monroe, and McMinn Counties came and few were disappointed. So many people swore they saw the murky form of the officer stride into the Sherold cabin and then disappear that, as a journalist noted, "Men are often hung on one-hundredth part of the evidence which substantiates this mystery."

The Sherolds could tolerate their uninvited visitor only for half a year. They moved out and the cabin was offered up for sale at bargain rates. There were no takers ("A Ghostly Tenant"). All these witnesses saw something—but what?

The residents of antebellum Monroe, Georgia, had long regarded the family—a man, a woman, and a daughter—who lived near the High Shoals Factory with suspicion. They were close-mouthed and isolated but admitted they were from Connecticut. It was rumored that the couple was not married. When the Civil War broke out, the family stayed put rather than return North. The man disappeared after Sherman's March to the Sea, and his wife claimed to have no idea where he went. Had he been murdered? Had he been abducted or killed by Sherman's camp followers? Had he abandoned his wife? Finally, the woman moved back to her native region, leaving the house empty and the mystery of the man's whereabouts unsolved.

The house was occupied by a succession of families, none of which stayed long. Some of them left in the middle of the night. They were driven to distraction by creepy noises emanating from the house, including the canonical moans and rattling chains, an indication that any spirits present were not blessed with great imaginations. In one room, persons heard a woman singing a lullaby; the peaceful song's mood was broken when the doors abruptly opened by themselves and observers heard the sound of people walking up and down the stairs. According to one account, "hundreds of reliable witnesses" heard the noises. Passersby would see lights in the windows that flickered out when the house was approached. The residence soon gained an unenviable reputation among locals and travelers, who were content to walk far out of their way to avoid it.

A prominent preacher who believed not in revenants spent the night in the house. Next morning the pale and shaken man said he wouldn't spend another night there "for all the gold in the universe." As of 1885, the last resident of the house was a man, old and full of days, who alone could bear the din of the unseen dead ("A Haunted House" 2).

In 1862, slave Silas Johnson helped his master bury \$11,000 worth of gold in the woods on the east bank of the Cumberland River near Nashville. Afterward, the master joined the Confederate army and was killed in Virginia. In July 1905, Johnson requested permission from the Nashville Board of Public Works to dig up the treasure, asserting that only he knew the exact spot. The permit was not granted, so for all we know the gold awaits discovery. A perhaps significant clue: Johnson specifically wanted to dig at the property occupied in 1905 by the Prewitt Spurr Manufacturing Company ("Says Master Buried..." 3).

It was said in Columbus, Georgia, that a local man buried gold and silver in a field 4 miles from town. By 1873, he was deceased, and among his papers was a cipher containing directions to the treasure. Excited searchers found a hole in the location indicated, but no gold or silver. Rumor held that the man's former slave located it ("Columbus, Ga." 2).

Treville Meche, who lived near Grand Coteau, Louisiana, buried an estimated \$800–1,000 worth of gold on his property during the war. He let his kin in on the location. Then he went paranoid, convinced someone outside the family knew the secret. So he dug up the gold and hid it elsewhere, but this time he didn't inform anyone where he put it. Then he lost his reason and became ill. He died on April 7, 1864. No one had any idea where the treasure was until March 1874, when laborers on the Meche homestead suddenly spent $400 in gold in Opelousas. They admitted they had plowed up the stash—or, at least, part of it ("Opelousas [LA] …" 2). Was the remainder ever found? The records don't tell us.

In November 1901, a farm tenant of J. B. Nealson's discovered four mysterious graves while hunting near Cluttsville, Alabama. The graves were quite old—the stone slabs were weatherbeaten and covered with moss, yet they bore no names. The oldest people in the territory could not remember anyone having been buried there, so the graves were opened. They contained not skeletons but treasure: oaken boxes full of silver cutlery, old-fashioned silver plate, and a nearly complete china service. A small tin box held a moldy cloth which, when unwrapped, disclosed $500 in gold coins. Who buried these things, and when? And why? No one could say, but likely some well-to-do person buried the family valuables for safekeeping during the Civil War, cleverly constructed false tombstones to throw marauders off the scent, and then failed to come back for it ("Treasure Found Buried in Mysterious Graves" 6).

H. C. Helm of Hickman, Kentucky, was hard at work in September 1916, tearing down his old house to make room for a new one. He had a double layer of flooring to take up, and when he removed the first tier, he discovered many bloodstains. During the late war, his house had been commandeered as a makeshift hospital ("Ghastly Reminder" 6).

Tombstone epitaph on Rebecca Jones Alford in Pleasant Grove Baptist Church Cemetery, Wake County, North Carolina: "A devoted Christian mother, who whipped Sherman's bummers with scalding water while they were trying to take her dinner pot, which contained a ham bone being cooked for her soldier boys" ("Epitaph Lauds..." 10).

In 1877 it was reported that a Virginia gravestone on two brothers, who had fought on opposing sides of the war, read: "God knows who was right" ("Major Thomas G. Jones…" 2).

A Boston newspaper correspondent saw this epitaph on a Union soldier in Newport News, Virginia, in early 1864: "Mustered Out" ("The correspondent…" 1).

When veteran James R. Jordan died at age ninety-four in Atlanta on March 11, 1937, his lengthy white hair was worth walking many a weary mile to see. The story behind it: he had once vowed never to cut his locks again "until the Confederacy is free," and Jordan was a man of his word ("Long-Haired Vet Dies" 1).

Laborers were digging behind the Hotel Miller in Macon, Missouri, in July 1904, when one man's shovel disappeared into a hole in the ground and nearly pulled him in with it. Investigation revealed a lengthy, forgotten tunnel extending from northwest to southeast and ending in a large underground room. It was supported by boards on the sides. Railroad ties served as a roof. Though clearly decades old, the tunnel was in good condition. Some theorized that it had been built to allow a means of escape if guerrilla Bloody Bill Anderson raided the Harris prison stockade ("More Tales Recalled by Discovery…" 7).

17
Multiracial Confederates

In the movies, the Southern troops are 100 percent white. Sometimes for variety you'll see a European in the ranks. But this is far from accurate. As we have seen, whites were not the only slaveowners in America, though many historians don't like to admit it and the average person on the street believes slavery was unknown in North America until Europeans "introduced" it.

Not only were many American Indians slaveowners, but many also fought for the Confederacy. Early in the war, the rebel government sent emissary Albert Pike to make treaties with Indian tribes. Pike raised troops among the Creek, Choctaw, and Cherokee in the autumn of 1860, several months before the war officially began, though it should be noted that many were disgruntled to find the military had arranged for neither their pay nor weapons (Garrison *More Civil* 194). In November 1861 the Confederacy established a Department of Indian Territory, and soon Indians were being actively recruited. As the war raged in Missouri in early 1862, four regiments and two battalions consisted of Indian soldiers; another regiment and several additional battalions were later formed. In late 1864 three major brigades were formed from this large number. In addition, a smattering of Indian soldiers served among white regiments (Wiley 324-25).

Approximately 8,500 Cherokee joined the Confederacy while 13,000 remained loyal to the Union ("Old Document Shows" 19). The Cherokee had representatives in the Confederate legislature and at least one North Carolina regiment, Company A of Thomas's Legion, consisted of Cherokee troops. A full-blooded Cherokee, Chief Stand Watie, was a member of a group called Knights of the Golden Circle, designed to defend states' rights and protect slavery. He eventually became a brigadier general in a Cherokee regiment he raised. On June 23, 1865, Watie became the last Confederate general to surrender his arms. In addition, the Creek, Choctaw, and Chickasaw tribes were overwhelmingly pro-Confederacy (Potter; Starkey 320; J. Harrison 61).

One unanticipated problem was that Watie's Cherokee soldiers were volunteers while another band was unwillingly drafted by the Confederacy. On one occasion, the two factions deliberately fired at each other in the heat of battle (Garrison *More Civil* 30-31).

By 1862 the Creek had formed two regiments, the Choctaw one, and the Chickasaw two battalions (Anderson 3). Other tribes known to have fought for the South, though perhaps not with the same enthusiasm, were the Osage and the Seminole (Wiley

325), who by the second year of the war had formed one battalion and one regiment respectively (Anderson 3). The Caddo and Arapaho near Fort Cobb formed a battalion and there was also at least one company of Comanche (Anderson 3). So many Catawba owned slaves and fought for the Confederacy that a monument to them was erected at Fort Mill, S.C., in August 1900 ("Monument to Indians" 3).

In 1860, Charleston, S.C., was home to eleven Indian families who owned slaves (Wilson 490). Many wealthy Cherokee fought for the Confederacy; however, they freed their slaves before the Confederacy did. At an 1863 meeting of the Cherokee Council at Cowskin Prairie, Indian Territory (Oklahoma), the Indians passed their own emancipation proclamation that "all Negro and other slaves within lands of the Cherokee Nation be and are hereby emancipated from slavery" ("Old Document Shows" 19). Violators were to be fined. Note the reference to "other" slaves; the Cherokee had some who weren't black, presumably Indians from other tribes.

Indians fought for the South at Wilson's Creek in the autumn of 1861, where their battle cries created "surprise, if not alarm" among the Federals. Cherokee troops from North Carolina fought at Baptist Gap in late 1862; the Confederate Indians won the battle and scalped some slain Union soldiers for good measure. Indians fought also at Honey Springs (July 1862) and at Camden, Arkansas (April 1864). The most important Civil War battle in which Indians fought in significant numbers was the Battle of Pea Ridge, Arkansas, March 6–8, 1862; some of the combatants employed traditional Amerindian weapons such as hatchets and bows and arrows. However, it was noted that the discipline of many Indian troops who engaged in the battle was poor (Wiley 325-26).

On the other hand, historian Bell Wiley relates that Indian soldiers' defection to the Union side was common. This may well have been because "[t]he Indian soldiers of the Confederacy were victims of shabby treatment by their white superiors.... [This] treatment of the Indians was, indeed, one of the darkest and most regrettable episodes of Confederate history" (325, 327). This probably did not come as a big surprise to the Indians. Nevertheless, they did fight for the Confederacy, a fact that is usually overlooked or ignored; they fought nobly in many instances; and despite "shabby treatment" some remained loyal to the Confederacy right to the very end. But not all. When the South's fortunes turned and it became obvious the Confederacy was doomed, the Cherokee decided to make no treaty with the South and kicked all secessionists out of their government ("Old Document Shows" 19).

There was considerable Hispanic support for the Confederacy. For example, Santos Benavides of Laredo, Texas, was a captain in the 33rd Texas Cavalry, which consisted largely of Hispanic troops. In November 1863 Benavides was promoted to colonel and raised his own regiment called the Partisan Rangers. They became known as "the Confederacy on the Rio Grande." On March 19, 1864, forty-two Confederates under Benavides successfully defended Laredo against an attack by 2,000 Union soldiers (Harrison 61; Thompson).

A Latina woman from New Orleans named Loreta Janeta Velasquez disguised herself as a man, called herself Harry T. Buford and became a lieutenant in the CSA. She served as a company commander under Brigadier General Bernard Bee at the First Battle of Bull Run/First Manassas (Garrison *More Civil* 97). Velasquez also fought at Ball's Bluff, Fort Pillow, and was wounded at Shiloh. Although her identity was eventually discovered, she continued to work for the South as a spy. After the war she wrote about her experiences.

In addition, it is often overlooked that the Confederate Secretary of the Treasury was Jewish: Judah Benjamin, who was twice elected a Louisiana senator after the war.

Even more counterintuitive is the presence of thousands of blacks who fought in some capacity for the South—and yes, many were free men. Not every rebel military outfit contained black soldiers; not all Southern blacks wanted to fight for the Confederacy; some were coerced into service; blacks were not all happily welcomed into military service by Confederate leaders. However, it is demonstrably true many blacks sympathized with their homeland (if not with the institution of slavery) and many did fight against the Union army. Pop culture may tell only part of the story, historians may downplay inconvenient contradictions to their version of events, and our own expectations may leave us in denial, but the facts are there.

Certainly, the Confederacy impressed many grudging blacks into military service. For example, a "bill authorizing the impressment of slaves and property for the use of the army" passed the Confederate Congress in February 1863 ("The bill authorizing the impressment..." 1). On July 10, 1863, the mayor of Charleston, S.C., issued a proclamation putting possibly unwilling blacks not in the military, but rather to labor on breastworks, by "impressing all free male Negroes and mulattos residing in that city between the ages of eighteen and sixty, and all able-bodied male slaves within the same, to finish the defenses of Morris Island" ("The Mayor of Charleston..." 1). The Confederate guerrilla R. V. Richardson planned to conscript all "light-colored Negroes" between the ages of eighteen and forty to serve three years as unvoluntary soldiers without pay, on the promise that they would be freed when their term expired ("The guerrilla Richardson..." 3). As of February 1864, "the impressment of able-bodied Negroes into the rebel armies is the subject of much controversy in the rebel press." This referred to a bill under debate in the Confederate Congress to impress all free black males between age eighteen and fifty to work on fortifications, prepare war materiel, or serve in military hospitals, for which they were to be paid $11 per month; ditto for a proposed 20,000 slaves, also to be paid, and their masters were to be compensated if any died in war or escaped ("The impressment..." 1; "On the following day..." 1). Note that by this time the Confederacy was willing to pay for their help.

(Incidentally, Federal forces also were known to force blacks to lend a hand to the war effort whether they liked it or not. Only a few weeks after Bull Run, Union Major General John E. Wool forced runaway slaves to build a redoubt at Fort Monroe; a railroad; roads and bridges. Secretary of War Simon Cameron heartily approved and wanted some of Wool's free laborers sent to General McClellan (Garrison *Civil War Curiosities* 257).)

On the other hand, many southern blacks fought with no coercion. Exactly how many served with the Confederates no one will ever know, but estimates range from 40,000 (Young 121) to 60,000 (Segars 3) to 93,000 (Shenkman and Reiger 106). Some were body servants who followed their masters into war—but the reader will note cases in which some remained with the military even after their masters were killed. Some historians minimize the significant role played by these body servants and other blacks in the Confederacy by dismissing them as "only" laborers, cooks, or teamsters; however, these occupations are crucial to the success of any army. Indeed, many black

Confederate body servants, cooks, hostelers, and teamsters qualified for pensions after the war (Jordan 64). And although many historians claim blacks who served with the CSA were used strictly as manual laborers, it is apparent that countless were full-fledged soldiers who carried weapons.

While it is true that "the official policy of the Confederate government prohibited blacks from serving as armed soldiers" until March 1865 (Bergeron 247), both slaves and free men took up arms despite official policy. It appears that commanders in the field were not averse to bending the rules involving their enlistment. A black historian, George Washington Williams, wrote in his 1882 *History of the Negro Race in America*: "From the earliest dawn of the war the rebel authorities did not frown upon the action of local authorities in placing arms in the hands of free Negroes" (qtd. in Jordan 66). Observe that Williams meant real weapons of war, not just shovels for digging trenches. For more evidence that blacks served in the Confederate military, consider an order issued in 1862 by Samuel Cooper, adjutant and inspector general for the CSA: "The adjutants of the regiments throughout the Army will inquire into and report all cases of slaves serving with their respective regiments without written authority from their masters" (Rollins "Servants" 76). Cooper didn't say slaves could not serve in the regiments, only that they were required to have written permission from their masters. Historians who claim there are few records of blacks serving in the CSA and therefore jump to the conclusion that their number has been exaggerated forget that many joined unofficially and therefore no records document their service. Then there is the fact that many records from the era are just lost. If not for eyewitness accounts, newspaper reports and post-war pension forms, there would be little evidence of their having fought at all.

The Tennessee legislature authorized the army's use of men of color as early as June 1861 (Rollins "Black Southerners" 2), only two months after the war began. Another source states that in May 1861, the Memphis Committee of Safety asked that three men, Deloach, Cook, and Greenlaw, "be authorized to organize a volunteer company composed of our patriotic free men of color of the city ... for the service of our common defense." The *Memphis Bulletin* in 1863 called this "the first attempt to arm the blacks in this war, and that too under the official sanction of a body of gentleman who, at the time, were the very embodiment of Southern chivalry, policy, and sentiment" ("Origin of Arming Negroes" 1). Very early in the war, a native of Charleston, S.C., observed "a thousand Negroes who, so far from inclining to insurrections, were grinning from ear to ear at the prospect of shooting Yankees" (Rollins "Black Southerners" 2). Therefore, many blacks fought at the beginning of the war, not just at the end, as is well known, when the Southern army was desperate to refill its ranks. Abolitionist Frederick Douglass confirms it. In the fall of 1861, just a few months after the commencement of the war, he was distressed that the Union army refused to recruit black soldiers while the Confederates did. He wrote:

> There are at the present moment, many colored men in the Confederate Army doing duty not only as cooks, servants, and laborers, but as real soldiers, having muskets on their shoulders and bullets in their pockets, ready to shoot down loyal troops and do all that soldiers may do to destroy the Federal government and build up that of the traitors and rebels. (qtd. in Harper 10)

In contrast, the Union army did not employ blacks as combat soldiers until 1863, when the famous 54th Massachusetts Regiment was formed. Incidentally, an unsettling detail that fails to appear in *Glory*, a film about the heroism of the 54th, is that when the troops attacked Fort Wagner, they met with resistance from at least one black Confederate soldier in the 1st South Carolina Artillery. His name was John Wilson Buckner, and he was wounded in action (Rollins "Black Southerners" 18).

The *New York Tribune* of December 25, 1861 (again, the first year of the war) contains a report from Fortress Monroe, datelined December 23, detailing the eye-opening experience of the 20th New York Regiment. After marching from Newport News, Virginia, the soldiers were fired upon near the Newmarket Bridge by 700 Confederate soldiers including "a whole company of Negroes ... two of our men are known to have been shot by them" ("From Fortress Monroe, the Late Skirmish" 5). On December 26, the *Tribune* printed another report from their correspondent at Fortress Monroe, at Hampton, Virginia, 10 miles from Newport News, who wrote: "It is well attested and beyond all dispute that a file of Negroes acted as infantry on the occasion, fired on our soldiers and probably wounded our men." He continued:

> I have taken considerable pains to ascertain the facts, and to settle, if possible, whether the Negroes were a regularly-organized corps, acting like other soldiers, or were merely camp-followers—servants of officers—appearing specially and "on that occasion only." Col. Weber inclines to the latter idea. It is asserted that the Negroes had something on their caps resembling lace. This would go at least as far to favor the idea that they were soldiers as that they were servants. Anything like uniformity in dress favors the theory of a distinct military organization. While the suggestion that the Negroes were but servants forced to play the soldiers on the occasion is a natural one, the evidence afforded by the uniform is inconsistent, and goes furthest to sustain the opposite conclusion. The indisputable fact that Negroes have been thus employed, that they have fired on our forces and wounded our men, has caused considerable feeling.... ("From Fortress Monroe, the Skirmish..." 5)

Although there was some ambiguity involving the blacks' outfits, the writer believed they were indeed soldiers, not servants. In any case, as he noted, they were shooting to kill Union troops.

Is there corroboration for this event? Perhaps. The *Indianapolis Star* printed a letter dated December 23, 1861, and written by a Union soldier near Newport News who seems to have been an eyewitness to the incident, since the date and place of the attack match the *Tribune's* report. Amazingly, the soldier claimed *all* the soldiers who fired at the Yankees were black. He wrote, "A body of seven hundred Negro infantry opened fire on our men, wounding two lieutenants and two privates. The wounded men testify positively that they were shot by Negroes, and that not less than seven hundred were present, armed with muskets" (Harper 21-2). The Union officers complained, "If they fight us with Negroes, then why should we not fight them with Negroes, too?... Let us fight the devil with fire" (Jordan 66).

Stonewall Jackson's Confederate Infantry at Frederick, Maryland, was estimated to contain as many as 3,000 blacks in 1862, still early in the war. Hard to believe, perhaps, but the figure came from Dr. Lewis Steiner, a chief inspector for the U.S. Army Sanitary

Commission. Were they all employed as trench-diggers, cooks, servants, or foragers? Not according to Dr. Steiner, who wrote: "Most of the Negroes had arms, rifles, muskets, sabres, bowie-knives, dirks, etc. ... and were manifestly an integral portion of the Southern Confederate Army" (Kennedy and Kennedy 90).

On May 18, 1862, a newspaper called the *Atlanta Confederacy* waxed enthusiastic on the prospect of arming blacks in the Confederate cause: "We must 'fight the devil with fire' by arming our Negroes to fight the Yankees. There is no doubt that in Georgia alone we could pick up ten thousand Negroes that would rejoice in meeting fifteen thousand Yankees in deadly conflict. We would be willing almost to risk the fate of the South upon such an encounter in an open field" ("A Proposition to Arm Negroes" 4).

In his 1963 study *The Civil War in Louisiana*, Professor John D. Winters estimated that 3,000 free blacks had volunteered to join militias by early 1862 (Bergeron 248). A *New York Times* reporter who rode with General Grant in 1863 reported seeing an artillery crew in Tennessee that was made up almost entirely of blacks (Rollins "Black Southerners" 20). Similarly, another *Times* reporter confirmed that black soldiers manned the rebel batteries at the Battle of Grand Gulf, Mississippi, "a single white man, or perhaps two, directing operations. There is no mistake on this point" ("Rebel [Negroes]" 1). A Union officer at Virginia's Rappahannock River reported in March 1863 that he saw a company of about fifty Confederate soldiers that included "Negroes [armed and uniformed], the same as white soldiers" (Jordan 67). Here is an irony to ponder. Northern black soldiers were kept segregated in their own units, while many eyewitness accounts of Southern black soldiers reveal that they fought alongside whites in the same regiments. The *New York Tribune* of December 26, 1861, complained:

> Black regiments are now fighting us side by side with the white rebels. They are used to escort our brethren who have been made prisoners of war on their way from one dungeon to another. They stood in line with whites (as is proclaimed on rebel authority) in a recent grand review of rebel soldiers at New Orleans. The traitors have thousands of such already in their ranks, and can increase them to hundreds of thousands at will. Any slave will put on a uniform and take a musket and drill at his master's word. ("Question Stated" 4)

Another witness was a British captain, Arthur Fremantle, who traveled with General Lee's army. On the Gettysburg campaign in 1863 he saw—among other acts of loyalty to the South—a black who guarded white Northern prisoners of war:

> This little episode of a Southern slave leading a white Yankee soldier through a Northern village, alone and of his own accord, would not have been gratifying to an abolitionist.... Nor would the sympathizers both in England and in the North feel encouraged if they could hear the language of detestation and contempt with which the numerous Negroes with Southern armies speak of their liberators. (Kennedy and Kennedy 91)

(Perhaps that "detestation and contempt" had its origin in the fact that Union soldiers were sometimes far crueler to Southern blacks than their masters ever had been. In October 1862 a reporter from Union-occupied New Bern, N.C., wrote to the *New York Tribune*: "The situation of the poor, unhappy blacks ... is such as should excite the sympathy of every Christian man. I am sorry to say that they are treated with great sternness and severity amounting to positive cruelty, by our own soldiers who seem to regard them as hardly better than beasts. Not a few of our officers conduct themselves in the most unfeeling manner toward these unfortunate creatures and are in fact ... expressing their hatred and contempt for the 'd-----d nigger'" (Harper 16). For specific examples of Northern atrocities toward both Southern blacks and whites, see Kennedy and Kennedy, chapter 4 and pp. 100-103, and Austerman 45.)

After the war, the U.S. Congress decreed that eligible former Confederate soldiers could receive pensions for their combat service. As we will see below, many were awarded to blacks.

Black educator Dr. Leonard L. Haynes stated confidently, "When you eliminate the black Confederate soldier, you've eliminated the history of the South" (qtd. in Jordan 57). And yet there are plenty of people who have wanted to do exactly that, including the federal government, which for years furnished free grave markers for both white and black Union veterans and white Confederate veterans, but refused to provide stones for black Confederates (Cartwright 95). As a result of these years of neglect and purposeful omission, black Confederates are, in the eloquent words of Ervin L. Jordan. Jr., "the Civil War's forgotten people, yet their existence was more widespread than American history has recorded. Their bones rest in unhonored glory in Southern soil, shrouded by falsehoods, indifference, and historians' censorship" (69).

Here are more specific examples of blacks you won't be reading about in school textbooks because they contradicted the way we think history should have been.

* The first major engagement of the war—known as the First Battle of Bull Run in the North and First Manassas in the South—took place on July 21, 1861. Eyewitness accounts reveal that even in this earliest battle "Black combatants shot, killed and captured Union troops." For example, an officer's servant in the 13th Arkansas Regiment died of wounds he received while fighting, and one Southern artillery battery contained four blacks. A Northern newspaper, the *Exchange*, confirmed for posterity that blacks enlisted in the CSA shot Union soldiers during the battle: "The war has dispelled one delusion of the abolitionists. The Negroes regard them as enemies instead of friends. No insurrection has occurred in the South—no important stampede of slaves has evinced their desire for freedom. On the contrary, they have jeered at and insulted our troops, have readily enlisted in the rebel army and on Sunday, at Manassas, shot down our men with as much alacrity as if abolitionism had never existed" (Harper 21).
* James Jefferson, a slave from Summerfield, Alabama, fought in both the first and one of the last battles of the war. His master was Dr. Samuel Vaughn; the doctor's son joined Company C, 4th Alabama Infantry, early in the war. Dr. Vaughn and Jefferson traveled to visit the son and arrived at his Virginia encampment on July 21, 1861, as the First Battle of Bull Run was starting. Although the doctor and his servant were only civilians on the battlefield, they seized muskets from wounded Confederate soldiers and helped fight off the Union army. Jefferson Davis personally congratulated James Jefferson after the battle.

  In the final days of the war, James Jefferson was one of the defenders who joined General Forrest's command during the Union siege of Selma on April 2, 1865. The

Civil War would end only a few days later. In his later years, James Jefferson received a Confederate pension (Cartwright 112-14).

* Private Henry Brown of Darlington, South Carolina, was a Confederate drummer. Later, a 15-foot monument was erected in his honor (Garrison *More Civil* 147-48).
* Remarkably, even before Bull Run "a black with the 1st Virginia Cavalry singlehandedly killed a Union soldier on July 2, 1861, during a skirmish at Falling Waters near Martinsburg" (Jordan 67).
* At Mechanicsville one white soldier refused to enter the battle. A servant named Westley asked for and received permission to fight in the soldier's place. A witness later recalled that "though Minié balls of the enemy were falling thick and fast about him, Westley never wavered, but brought down a Yankee at every fire" (Rollins "Black Southerners" 14). Writer Richard Rollins provides several other examples of servants and cooks fighting the enemy under battle conditions.
* The Confederate Navy contracted a bridge engineer from Alabama, Horace King, to build warships. He was a former slave (Sons of Confederate Veterans). Throughout the war King donated money to the war effort and sent uniforms and money to the fighting sons of his former master (Rollins "Black Southerners" 8).
* Holt Collier enlisted in a Mississippi regiment. In 1902 he was wrongly called "the only colored man regularly enlisted in the Confederate Army." He became Theodore Roosevelt's guide when the president went bear hunting ("About Holt Collier" 10).
* Amos Rucker and his master Cornelius Sample joined Company C, 63rd Georgia. In later years he was a fixture at Confederate reunions. At the one held in Louisville in June 1905, Rucker said lots of things that would not pass muster today, for example, that he loved the Confederate flag and wished he could fight for it again ("Grizzled" 5). Rucker's opinions make us uncomfortable, but he wasn't shy about expressing them. When he died in Atlanta in October 1905, the Camp W. H. T. Walker Chapter of the United Sates Confederate Veterans—of which he was a member—were his pallbearers ("Confederates Do Honor" 1).
* The 1st Regiment Louisiana Native Guards were a Confederate militia regiment consisting of some 1,500 free black men from New Orleans (Bergeron 247-248). That's quite a number of people to sweep under the rug of history.
* During the siege of Yorktown from April 5 to May 4, 1862, "several of the Confederacy's best sharpshooters were Afro-Virginians" (Jordan 67).
* A company of blacks served with the 3rd and 4th Georgia Regiments. Seventy blacks in Lynchburg, Tennessee, enlisted to fight right after Virginia seceded. The 3rd Alabama Infantry contained 1,000 white soldiers, and nearly 1,000 black soldiers. And the 6th Louisiana Cavalry included at least nine blacks "and probably many more" (Rollins "Black Southerners" 2-3; 10; 22).
* Julia Mason of Mississippi, a twenty-one-year-old black woman, was a nurse for Captain Moffett's Louisiana regiment. She paid a dear price for supporting the South when her arm was shot off on Grove Street during the siege of Vicksburg in July 1863. She applied for a pension in 1899 (Cotton D4). Similarly, Monroe Jones, who served with the 1st Mississippi Artillery, lost both legs during a shell attack at Vicksburg. Also, James Mackey, who "had been in the war since it started, serving for Henry Butler" had his right arm shattered below the elbow by an exploding shell. Around 1984, a file of applications for Confederate pensions was discovered

in Vicksburg. This included thirty applications from former slaves, including Mason, Jones, and Mackey. Most of the applications were approved (Cotton D4).

* "Confederate Mary" was a spy for the South. She crossed enemy lines many times, bringing back valuable information and medicine for the troops (Rollins "Black Southerners" 13).
* A free black woman, Hattie Carter, was an ammunition runner for the CSA in Richmond, Virginia. (Rollins "Black Southerners" 18).
* According to the *Religious Herald* of September 10, 1863, a white Tennessee regiment had, by their own request, a black chaplain called Uncle Lewis (Harper 25). He served with them until the end of the war.
* A black woman named Betsey Fuller in Norfolk, Virginia, owned her slave husband. He "was an ardent secessionist and was in full sympathy with the firing on Fort Sumter. After Norfolk was evacuated and was occupied by the federal forces [in 1862], he was loud in his expression of Southern views and was at one time in the chain gang because of opinions obnoxious to the military" (Wilson 488; Jordan 65).
* Approximately 500 slaves accompanied the 8th Texas Cavalry. These slaves "repeatedly proved their worth to the greycoats" (Austerman 42).
* When Confederate General John Hunt Morgan of Lexington, Kentucky, made his surprise raids in Indiana and Ohio in the summer of 1863, his cavalry was accompanied by scores of armed blacks. Morgan's own servant, a man known as "Old Box," was a "fanatical Confederate" who refused to heed the general's urgings that he should head for Union territory while the outfit was in the heat of battle (Austerman 43-4).
* George Mills of Henderson County, N.C., was a slave who went to war alongside his master, Captain Walter Bryson. When Bryson was killed at Sharpsburg, Maryland, in September 1862, Mills sought his master's body on the battlefield, purchased a wrought-iron casket, and traveled by train and wagon to send Bryson home for burial. Mills was set free in Bryson's will. What did he do with his new freedom? Did he head North and join the Union army? No, Mills joined the Confederate army as a soldier, and he served for the duration of the war. Until his death in 1926 at age 83, Mills was an active member of the Confederate Veterans' Association. When descendants of Captain Bryson gathered at Hendersonville to honor the memory of George Mills in June 1999, Bryson's great-great-grandnephew remarked: "When you read some of the history of the period, they tend to make the conflict sound so clear-cut. We forget that they were complex, full-rounded individuals with friends, family, and [were] people who were willing to do this" ("Black Confederate" M5).
* A Canton, Mississippi, cemetery contains a large obelisk raised to commemorate the black soldiers who fought with a unit called "Harvey's Scouts," which was attached to General Nathan B. Forrest's cavalry in 1864 (Rollins "Black Southerners" 4). After the war, Forrest was full of praise for his black troops. In August 1868 he told a reporter for the *Cincinnati Commercial* that "these boys stayed with me, drove my teams, and better Confederates did not live." In a similar vein, Forrest told the *Louisville Courier-Journal* in 1869 that the black supporters of the Confederacy "behaved in such a manner that I shall always respect them for it ... I have always felt kind toward them and always treated them kindly." Author Thomas Cartwright provides a long list of black soldiers who fought under Forrest and later applied

for pensions, along with testimonials from whites who served with them (95, 115, *passim*).

* Eli Dempsey, a black who fought with the 1st North Carolina Artillery, was captured in 1862 and held as a POW for two years (Rollins "Black Southerners" 12).
* In 1986, Arthur W. Bergeron, Jr., examined the military careers of fifteen free blacks who fought as privates in regular Confederate units. He found that "[t]welve of these men enlisted in Louisiana volunteer regiments, two in a home guard or reserve unit, and one in a Texas cavalry unit. Three of the first twelve fought in several battles, and two of the three received wounds" (248). Bergeron concludes his study:

> The actions of these free blacks seem to argue for what may be to some an unpopular conclusion. By volunteering for combat duty in regular Confederate service, these men took what can be seen as the final step of their acceptance or acculturation into the local white societies where they lived.... [In certain Louisiana parishes] many whites and free blacks must have enjoyed a freedom of association that has received relatively little attention by social scientists. The actions of these free men of color in volunteering for—and of their white comrades in accepting them into military units— should lead us to take a closer look at race relations in Louisiana's pre-Civil War period. (255)

* One of the men Bergeron studied was Charles F. Lutz, a light-skinned free man of color who served as a soldier in the 8th Louisiana Volunteer Infantry, Company F. He enlisted on June 23, 1861—again, near the beginning of the war. He fought in several major battles in Virginia and became a prisoner of war at the Battle of Second Fredericksburg on May 3, 1863. Two weeks later he was released during a prisoner exchange but was wounded at Gettysburg on July 2. He became a POW for a second time, was again exchanged in September for a Northern prisoner, then furloughed after performing such meritorious duty (248-49). He was awarded a pension in 1900.
* Levy Carnine served as his master's bodyguard when the latter joined the Pelican Rifles, part of the 2nd Louisiana Volunteer Regiment, in 1861. When his master was killed in battle, Carnine had him buried and remained with the regiment. He volunteered to serve as bodyguard for the outfit's colonel until the colonel himself was slain. Again, Carnine saw to the burial. Now entirely without a master, Carnine could have fled North. Instead, he again "took up with the boys" in the Pelican Rifles regiment in Virginia, even joining them in battle. At one point he gathered money and mail from the soldiers and delivered it to their families in Louisiana. To do this, Carnine had to cross enemy lines. After his successful (and very dangerous) mission, he joined a newly formed regiment and served as a bodyguard for one of his late master's relatives. For his efforts he was named an honorary member of the United Confederate Veterans and upon his death, Carnine was buried in Mansfield, Louisiana, among former members of the CSA (Kennedy and Kennedy 94-6).
* By studying a few sample pension forms filled out by black CSA veterans in Tennessee, Richard Rollins found numerous instances of their being wounded in combat. A few examples: Henry Neal and Taylor Kinnard were shot in the left leg and the arm, respectively, at Shiloh; Ned McCullough was wounded at Murfreesboro and Chattanooga; Ike Anderson was shot in the leg by Union soldiers and captured at Fort Donelson; Alfred Brown was wounded twice at Chickamauga (Rollins "Servants" 81).

* General Sherman's Union troops captured several blacks who apparently had been firing at them at Griswoldville, Georgia, in July 1864 (J. Harrison 62).
* Just after the Battle of Gettysburg, the *New York Herald* reported: "Among the rebel prisoners... there were observed seven Negroes in uniform and fully accoutered as soldiers" (Rollins "Black Confederates" 135).
* At the end of the war, "twenty-eight blacks surrendered and insisted on being paroled at Appomattox with Lee's army rather than accepting freedom" (Jordan 68).
* After the war, "a large number of black Southerners ... were allowed to attend United Confederate Veterans meetings." For example, the program for a 1905 U.C.V. reunion in Georgia lists five black veterans in attendance, and notes that all had seen active service (Cartwright 96; Lunsford 98).
* At the U.C.V. meeting in Louisville in June 1900, one attendee was Jerry Perkins of Brownsville, Tennessee, "[c]lad in an old suit of gray which he had proven his right to wear." He had followed his master Charlie Perkins into the 31st Tennessee Infantry and retrieved his body under heavy fire when he was killed early in the conflict. After accompanying his master's body home, Jerry returned to the unit and "serv[ed] with them gallantly and faithfully" until they surrendered at Greensboro in May 1865. He requested that he be buried with his comrades and they agreed ("Comrade Jerry" 7).
* Charley Sheppard entered the war as his master's valet, but he proudly considered himself a Confederate soldier. Evidently his comrades agreed; after he died on August 7, 1900, he was buried in the Confederate cemetery at Union City, Tennessee ("A Negro Confederate").
* "Uncle Bob" Smith died at his home near Glasgow, Kentucky, on September 7, 1910. His obituary condescendingly referred to him as "an old-time darkey [who] was highly esteemed by the white people." But it also mentioned that Smith was "a Confederate soldier" ("Negro Confederate Soldier Dies" 3).
* Daniel Hoggard of Providence, Kentucky, went to war as a servant of his master. When elderly he attended a reunion at the L. B. Hall Camp of Confederate Veterans ("Negro Confederate Veteran" 6).
* Josh Robinson was a slave of the Ewing Robinson family in Warren County, Kentucky. One day, as he was returning home with a sack of meal, he met Capt. Bassett, "who asked him if he did not want to join the army." Robinson flung the meal sack aside and enlisted immediately. He took care of the horses but also "shouldered a musket." He saw action at Chickamauga and the Battle of Cumberland Gap and was wounded at least once. He met Stonewall Jackson and shook hands with Jefferson Davis. Later he became the only black man to receive the Southern Cross of Honor from the United Daughters of the Confederacy. He also drew a Confederate pension (the press noted, erroneously, that he was "the only Negro who does"). In his old age, Robinson lived in Morganfield. He attended every reunion he could, and at each carried the banner of the Adam Johnson Company, the 10th Kentucky. Robinson expressed a wish to be buried in his Confederate uniform with his Southern Cross of Honor ("Draws Confederate Pension" 1).
* William Pete Wheeler of Paris, Kentucky, was a cook and bodyguard for Gen. Joseph Wheeler. Decades after the war, he was admitted to the Confederate Home in Oldham County ("Gen. Wheeler's Bodyguard" 6).
* Alf Whiting, "one of the few surviving Negroes who served in the Confederate army," was attached to Company K, 13th Virginia Infantry. He was captured and refused

to take the oath of allegiance to the federal government. Whiting died at Ronsey, Virginia, in March 1922; he requested that his pallbearers be fellow Confederate veterans. They complied ("Ex-Negro Slave" 12).

* Many years after the war, a debate arose in the Mississippi legislature as to whether a monument should be raised in Jackson to the Confederate dead. Republican John F. Harris, a former slave and delegate from Washington County, made a speech in support of the monument on February 11, 1890:

> I went with [the Confederate soldiers]. I, too, wore the gray, the same color my master wore. We stayed four long years, and if that war had gone on till now, I would have been there yet.... I want to honor those brave men who died for their convictions. When my mother died I was a boy. Who, sir, then acted the part of a mother to the orphaned slave boy, but my "old missus?" Were she living now, or could speak to me from those high realms where are gathered the sainted dead, she would tell me to vote for this bill. And sir, I shall vote for it.

Harris did vote for the memorial, as did every other black member of the legislature (Kennedy and Kennedy 107-09).

Many blacks, both slave and free, who did not take up arms and fight showed their support for the Confederacy in other ways:

* In Richmond, Virginia, a group of black musicians donated the proceeds from one of their concerts to the war effort. They called themselves the Confederate Ethiopian Serenaders (Rollins "Black Southerners" 2).
* Blacks in Fort Smith, Arkansas, and Vicksburg, Mississippi, sponsored balls to raise money for soldiers (Rollins "Black Southerners" 4).
* Other black Southerners donated cash and goods. For example, in Helena, S.C., they raised $90; a free black in Columbus, Georgia, contributed $300 to a Confederate loan; and a New Orleans real estate broker donated $500. Free black women in Savannah made uniforms. On the other end of the economic spectrum, one slave in Alabama gave a regiment a bushel of his sweet potatoes (Rollins "Black Southerners" 4).
* A black farmer in Fairfax County, Virginia, sold 28 acres of his land and donated the money to the state's defense (Jordan 59).
* A slave bugler named Lewis was denied permission to enlist in the 3rd Virginia Cavalry. Undaunted, he gave the regiment his bugle and $20 in cash (Jordan 59).
* The *Charleston Mercury* of April 24, 1861, relates that "a group of colored men offered to aid in building defenses and was put to work." On April 30 the same paper reported that "a company of colored men offered their services in Nashville, Tennessee" (Young 121). The significant word in both instances is offered.
* Isaac Cansler, a Baptist preacher of Lincolnton, N.C., grew poppies for the Confederacy's medicinal use (Young 122).
* David Deas, a Confederate scout, became a wealthy cotton buyer after the war. He died in Savannah in January 1872 ("David J. Deas..." 2).
* The *Greensborough* [N.C.] *Patriot* of May 7, 1861, reprints a story from the *Richmond Dispatch* concerning fifty-three free blacks of Amelia County, Virginia, who offered themselves "to the government for any service." An additional 200 free men from Petersburg volunteered "to fight under white officers, dig ditches, or anything that could show their desire to serve old Virginia" (Harper 9).

* In August 1862, several Montgomery, Alabama, blacks showed their support by donating sixty dollars' worth of watermelons to Confederate soldiers (Harper 12).
* Henry Jones of Clarksville, Virginia, donated $465 in gold to the Confederate treasury in August 1863 (Harper 12).
* The *Fayetteville* [N.C.] *Observer* of February 27, 1865, reports that blacks in Louisburg, Virginia, treated local Confederate soldiers to a feast (Harper 12).
* In November 1862, eighteen blacks in Savannah, Georgia, donated $90 to aid Georgia soldiers fighting in Virginia. The previous April, other black philanthropists gave seventy-two pairs of socks to a Georgia regiment (Harper 12).
* In New Bern, N.C., in May 1861, blacks donated 2,000 pounds of scrap metal for use in the manufacture of cannonballs (Harper 13).
* A black guide intentionally misled Union General Dahlgren into going in the wrong direction as his army headed for Richmond, Virginia, to support General Kilpatrick. As a result, Kilpatrick failed to take the city. The guide was hanged ("Treachery of a Negro Guide" 1).

Some blacks felt moved to show support for the Confederacy even many years after the CSA crumbled into ashes. When the Committee of the Confederate Veterans planned a reunion in 1901, the second largest individual contribution—a $1,000—came from Robert Church, a slave in his youth who became the wealthiest black citizen of Memphis ("Gives $1,000" 2; "A Former Slaves Gives" 4).

Bill Yopp, a former slave who lived in Macon, Georgia, visited the old Confederates at the Atlanta Soldiers' Home every Christmas and brought gifts for all—partly paid for by himself, partly by donations. In 1919 the Georgia Legislature passed a special fund to continue Yopp's work ("A Real Christmas Story" 6).

Despite orders from the Grand Army of the Republic, in June 1874 black citizens of Paducah, Kentucky, reportedly decorated the graves of the Confederate dead at Mound City ("Paducah *Kentuckian...*" 2).

As noted, some historians are quick to downplay the role played by Confederate blacks. One historian/sociologist's book mentions that many blacks betrayed the Confederacy, while not mentioning that many others showed unwavering support. The author mentions Southern blacks who were Union spies while neglecting to mention the ones who were Confederate spies. He mentions that blacks were not allowed to officially enlist in the Confederate army until three weeks before the war ended, but as we have seen, thousands of blacks enlisted anyway, right from the very beginning of the conflict, and a full two years before the Union army followed suit. He claims that "[m]ost of the many slaves who accompanied their owners were limited to performing menial tasks like foraging for food, washing laundry and throwing up earthworks" without acknowledging either the military usefulness of these chores or the fact that free blacks sometimes volunteered to do these things. He mentions the fact that thousands of slaves fled to territory occupied by the Union (Loewen 273-79), but it is also true that many slaves refused to do so, and some who ran away quickly came back home after being ill-treated by Northerners.

These wartime blacks served in the military both officially and unofficially, suffered great hardship, lost their property, lost their limbs, lost their homes, lost their relatives and lost their lives—but only because whites told them to do it? Even the free blacks?

Even the slaves who had the opportunity to join the Union army and refused? Are we to assume they were too passive to act or think on their own volition?

Indubitably blacks who sided with the South fought out of loyalty to their homes, their families and sometimes even out of friendship with their masters, not to keep slavery alive as an institution. (On the other hand, that may well have been an inducement for slave-owning free blacks—there were many, and like Indians who owned slaves, they too have been swept under history's rug.) Given that people often have numerous and indiscernible motives for the things they do, it's not far-fetched to conclude that most blacks who supported the Confederacy did so because they wanted to. We should remember a comment made in the *Civil War News* of August 1991 by Edward Smith, dean of minority affairs and professor of history at Washington's American University: "To admit that blacks actually fought for a cause which in the minds of many 20th century Americans now stands exclusively for slavery and oppression is unacceptable to many in the country concerned with only politics and not with the realities of historical record" (qtd. in Segars 1).

There are two angles—or more—to every historical argument. For a fact offered by one side, there seems to be an equally cogent opposing fact countered by the other side. Does this mean both sides are wrong? It would be more accurate to say both sides are correct within limitations. The truth, as usual, lies somewhere in between. This is not to say the standard view of history is totally wrong, only that it is incomplete, and the other side should not be flagrantly ignored or rejected out of hand just because it complicates a narrative.

18

Grave Robbers and Souvenir Hunters

At the time of the Civil War, body snatchers unearthed and stole the recently dead to sell to medical schools whose students desperately needed cadavers to dissect. That was the partially commendable motive. Others stole bodies sheerly for financial gain. Naturally, when the mortality rate skyrocketed due to the war, resurrectionists put their feelings of patriotism aside and lurked in the graveyards' shadows, pick and shovel in hand.

In November 1863, the graveyard near the Soldiers' Home in Washington, D.C., was robbed of bodies. Most intelligent snatchers were content to steal corpses and leave the grave's surface looking as undisturbed as possible to avoid detection, but this lot uprooted coffins, not just bodies, and had to abandon the former in the forests near the nation's capital, which suggests they were amateurs ("A profound feeling of horror..." 1).

If you ever visit the Camp Chase Confederate Cemetery in Columbus, Ohio, keep in mind that many of the soldiers who allegedly are there are not. In November 1864, many graves were systematically opened to supply a Cleveland medical school with cadavers. One physician, Dr. Flowers, was arrested on charges of trafficking in the dead ("Resurrectionists" 1).

After the war, a woman from Tennessee traveled to Chicago to locate the remains of her son, who had died at the Camp Douglas prison camp. She had never been outside the confines of her home county and made a sensation in the big city as she smoked a stubby pipe and wore fashions from sixty years before, not unlike Mammy Yokum. At the cemetery, she beseeched gravediggers to open the alleged resting place of her son. All were mortified when the grave proved empty, the target of resurrectionists. The body within had been "carved into shreds by the priests and acolytes of Aesculapius," as a reporter with a taste for classical allusions said ("Camp Douglas" 3).

Swiping Confederate bodies was so common in Chicago, in fact, that Union authorities asked the city's chief of police to crack down on body snatching. This practical worthy replied, "If I ever have to have an arm amputated, I'd rather it be cut off by a doctor who had had previous experience operating on a dead person. Besides, if they don't snatch Rebs, they'll just get Yanks" ("Camp Douglas" 3).

Then there were the tomb robbers whose motives were entirely greedy. They wanted to steal Civil War artifacts which even then were valuable collectors' items. As early as April 1895, residents of Missionary Ridge near Chattanooga were angered to find that someone had excavated mounds on the battlefield near what was once General Braxton Bragg's headquarters. That someone was disrespectful relic hunters, who had deprived the Confederate dead of their buttons, canteens, and worst of all, skulls and bones ("Desecrating Soldiers' Graves" 6). These relics may exist yet in private collections and museums.

A sensational trial involving the robbing of soldiers' graves unfolded in August 1898—sensational because the ghouls were soldiers themselves, so they faced not a civil trial but a court-martial. It all began when Captain L. C. Duncan from the 22nd Kansas was charged with robbing the tomb of Confederate Major Duke at Bull Run. The Kansas division was allied with the 3rd New York Infantry, a member of which related to the press that Duncan allegedly had stolen a sword, a watch, and even shoulder straps. The writer blamed it on "the craze for relics which has taken possession of the men around the battlefields of the rebellion" ("Court-Martial Trial" August 12, 1898 2).

A witness at the court-martial, Captain George Ross of Company I, testified that he caught Duncan and a dozen others in the act of "digging up rebels," which Duncan lamely tried to explain away by saying he was conducting medical research and wanted bones "to ascertain what the men in the graves had died from." (An educated guess: mostly disease or battle injuries, but very few cases of death from obesity or old age.) Ross immediately reported their activities. In addition, Sergeant J. M. Southerd saw a party of men handling such items as a human jawbone, uniform buttons, and epaulets ("Court-Martial Trial" August 16, 1898, 3).

On August 16, Corporal Adolph Gongal corroborated Ross's testimony, stating that he saw a Private Wise spading away on a Bull Run grave. Some soldiers were seen yanking teeth out of a skull. Another private testified that he overheard Duncan remarking, "This is the first grave I ever helped open in the daytime"—suggesting that he had opened others under the concealing mantle of darkness ("A Corporal's Evidence" 4).

The prosecution finished its case on August 18. Captain Duncan was in big trouble if found guilty, as grave robbing was a felony in Virginia ("Evidence All Heard" 2). When defense witnesses spoke, it was noted that their testimony was more hurtful than otherwise to Duncan. "It is said that the witnesses for the defense already examined have not improved Captain Duncan's case very much and have been of material aid to the prosecution" ("The Grave-Robbing Case" 5). It came as no surprise when Duncan was found guilty on August 29, but officers in the War Department were shocked when his punishment was fixed at only two months in the regimental camp, a formal reprimand, and a loss of half of his pay for two months. It was noted that when his "punishment" ended, Duncan could also be tried again under Virginia law ("Duncan is Guilty" 4). Undoubtedly the state would have thrown the book at him, but there is no evidence he faced a second trial. Only one of his assistants, Lieutenant Guy Morgan, appears to have also faced a court-martial, and he was acquitted on September 9 ("Acquitted of Desecrating Graves" 10).

Souvenir collectors' raiding of Civil War soldiers' graves still occurs from time to time, though it is a felony punishable with serious jail time. For years an unknown person had been buried with only a field rock as a marker in the Milburn-Travillion family cemetery on a mountain in Laurel County, Kentucky, allegedly a victim of the Battle of Wildcat Mountain, which occurred on October 21, 1861. On March 25, 1976, folks who lived nearby noticed a yawning hole in the cemetery. Investigators discovered that someone had dug all the way down to the coffin but, for some reason, did not open it. Surely it wasn't for lack of nerve. Deputy Sheriff Marshall Begley tapped the shallow dirt with a stick and heard it thumping against the wooden lid. Begley had no court order to see if the remains were there, so police shoveled the soil back in the grave.

But a week later, the would-be robber struck the same grave again. Sheriff James Yaden got a court order, and police found that the second time around the ghoul had refilled the grave but left a casket hinge on the surface. Digging revealed that the thief had carried away the entire casket, leaving behind only that hinge, the coffin handles and a beer can used to slake his thirst as he defiled a sacred resting place. Begley noted that the few pieces of casket remaining were made of American chestnut, an almost indestructible wood, which meant that the stolen body, whoever it was, was probably in good condition (Woolley D5).

The grave robber was never caught, and the body neither recovered nor identified. So who was the removed one? We shall never know, most likely, but there were a few clues. A chestnut casket would have been expensive; the abandoned handles were "fancy"; and a few pieces of glass found in the grave suggested that the casket had a window for viewing the remains. All of this suggests that the corpse had been prosperous.

In fact, if the grave robber were in search of Civil War souvenirs, he was badly disappointed. Those killed at Wildcat Mountain were removed from the cemetery shortly after the war ended and reburied at Zollicoffer National Cemetery in Nancy, Kentucky. Therefore, the pricey casket likely contained a civilian, not a soldier.

19

Legally Selling Humans: After the Civil War

Author's note: some of the following information appeared in slightly different form in my book *Forgotten Tales of Kentucky*.

At one time paupers and vagrants legally could be sold into servitude. They often were sold at auction by the authorities, just like slaves, and it was a common practice all over the USA. One supposes that it was marginally better than the British custom of sending them to debtor's prison.

On July 27, 1818, Lewis Cass, Democratic governor of the Michigan Territory, issued "An Act for the Punishment of Idle and Disorderly Persons," allowing such undesirables to be given ten lashes with a whip or sold by local constables into three months' servitude. Not only that, the law also applied broadly to "stubborn servants," prostitutes, brawlers, users of foul language, lewd persons, people "who misspend what they earn," individuals who wouldn't provide for their families, thieves, and "common drunkards"—maybe uncommon ones were let off the hook ("Whipping and Selling Poor White Men…" 3). The December 1, 1821, issue of the periodical *Niles' Register* records one result of Cass's law: a black man had recently purchased a white pauper at a Detroit auction and ordered him, "Follow your master." The vagrant walked after his owner to the docks, where the purchaser kindly bought him a steamboat ticket and sent him on his way ("The Tables Turned" 214). Memories of the draconian law came back to haunt Cass when he ran for president in 1848. Then observers recalled that an earlier president, William Henry Harrison, had passed similar laws when he was the first governor of the Indiana Territory and again when in the Ohio Senate ("Whipping and Selling Poor White Men…" 3).

In 1835, the Democratic Missouri Legislature passed a pauper-selling bill under the approval of Governor Dunklin. The law was taken seriously. In March 1840, the editor of the *St. Louis Republican* witnessed a white vagrant sold to a livery stable owner for $1 ("The editor…" 2).

An advertisement in the Middletown, Connecticut, *Sentinel* of February 3, 1837: "NOTICE: The poor of the Town of Chatham will be SOLD on the first Monday in April 1837, at the house of T. Penfield, Esq., at 9 o'clock in the forenoon" ("We copy the following…" 2). The state law was said to be "falling into disrepute" as of March 1853 ("Pauper Auctions"2).

Tennessee law *circa* 1840 authorized "the sale of vagrants and idlers to the highest bidder." The *Louisville Journal*'s editor wondered if this conceivably meant that black men could buy white men ("An Answer Expected" 2). As we have seen and shall see, in other states, at least, they could and did.

On June 4, 1843, two white men were sold in Spartanburg, South Carolina, for either debt, pauperism, or as punishment for crime. They went for a bargain 6.5 cents each and were considered too expensive even at that price ("Selling White Men" 2).

A white man was sold for vagrancy in Ogle Country, Illinois, around June 1853. He went for 25 cents, but the purchaser didn't have exact change, so his new slave loaned it to him ("A white man was sold for vagrancy…" 2).

A fellow named Garrett Davis, a member of the Know Nothing political party, was indicted for vagrancy in Bracken County, Kentucky, convicted, and sold into slavery for three months in November 1855 ("A Know-Nothing Vagrant" 2). After that, perhaps, the Know Nothing knew something—the importance of getting a job.

In May 1857, Andy Herrod, the jailer of Covington, Kentucky, purchased Mr. Hughes, described as a "miserable vagrant ... a poor sot of a fellow," though blessed with an industrious wife. Herrod got five months' worth of Hughes's labor for $1. "We are happy to say Herrod will make a kind master," remarked the *Cincinnati Gazette*, "although the law allows [Herrod] the same rights as the master of a Negro slave has" ("Price of a White Man" 3).

Jane McManus, a denizen of Louisville in the late 1850s, was famous in the city for her belligerence, fighting skills, and because she spent most of her time in the workhouse. Such was her reputation as a street brawler that the police nicknamed her War Eagle. She was arrested for fracturing the skull of Mary Fitzpatrick on January 11, 1858 ("Once More" 2). The attending physician's diagnosis was that Fitzpatrick would probably recover "if she don't kill herself with bad whisky"; others wished openly that her spirit would take flight already ("Police Court" January 15, 1858 1). In October, McManus, three other women, and a man named Charles Yater were convicted of vagrancy. According to statute law, the highest bidder could buy them for a year's servitude. The *Louisville Courier* noted that the quintet had a hard-won reputation for degradation, prostitution, thievery, and reluctance to reform, adding, "Whoever purchases the worthless creatures will procure a hard bargain" ("Four Woman and One Man…" 1). The fates of the five arrestees were debated in court ("Vagrant Question" 28 Oct. 1858 1). On October 30 came the announcement that Judge Muir discharged the women but also ruled that the sheriff must sell Yater into servitude for one year; the local press described Yater as an "unfortunate specimen of the Caucasian race" ("Vagrant Question" October 30, 1858 1; "Criminal Court" 1). Yater was sold for $1 in front of the courthouse on November 13 ("White Man Sold" 1), but evidently didn't learn his lesson. He was arrested for vagrancy again on May 11, 1860 ("Police Court" May 14, 1860 1). As for Jane McManus, the *Courier* gave her a surprisingly touching sendoff when she died in Cincinnati in August 1859: "Jane was an abandoned woman, and the vilest of her class, but she wouldn't lie. She had an eye like an eagle, the strength and courage of an Amazon, and the fierceness of a wildcat.... The War Eagle has taken her last flight and soars far beyond 'the valley of the shadow of death'" ("The Eagle's Last Flight" 1).

In the same month of War Eagle's demise, eight more Louisvillians were tried on vagrancy charges, five women and three men. Once again, a judge was lenient with the women and dismissed them, while ordering the three men (Pres Means, George Barker, and Caleb West) sold into servitude ("Mean Specimens" 1).

Parker Sheldon once was one of Maine's most prominent businessmen, a member of the state legislature, on the executive council, collector of the port of Bath, and the first mayor of Gardiner. But when he became old, senile, and feeble, he could no longer support himself and was sold at public auction around January 1858 ("Change of Circumstances" 1). On the other side of the coin, it was reported in March 1858 that an unnamed man in New Bedford, Massachusetts, who once had been so poor that he was sold as a vagrant, was now worth $150,000. Modern equivalent, over $5 million ("Life's Changes" 1).

The reader will note that all these incidents occurred before the Civil War. So when were human beings no longer sold at auction in the USA? Almost everyone thinks the practice ceased after the war, when Congress passed the Thirteenth Amendment to the Constitution, which officially abolished slavery, in December 1865. But it appears that few have read the Thirteenth Amendment very closely.

Consider the case of John Hanson, a black vagrant sold into servitude at auction in front of the Louisville, Kentucky, courthouse. Dick Zable, a vault cleaner, made the highest bid. For $2, Zable had the legal right to own Hanson for the period of one year, "subject to the law which governs the contract between apprentice and master." Zable put Hanson to work tending his horses. After the sale there was serious talk of auctioning off a white vagrant named Mack ("The Sale of a Vagrant" 6).

When did the auctioning of Hanson occur? On June 14, 1882—seventeen years after the war ended and the passing of the Thirteenth Amendment.

The national press condemned the act but in fact, as the *New York Sun* pointed out, it was perfectly legal. "The recent sale," said the paper, "... has surprised many persons who were not aware or had forgotten that the Constitution of the United States distinctly recognizes the lawfulness of slavery or involuntary servitude as a punishment for crime" ("Slavery as a Punishment for Crime" 2).

Section One of the Thirteenth Amendment reads (italics added): "Neither slavery nor involuntary servitude, *except as a punishment for crime whereof the party shall have been duly convicted*, shall exist within the United States, or any place subject to their jurisdiction." In other words, as the *Sun* put it:

> There is nothing in the constitutional prohibition to prevent a State from making slavery the penalty for very trivial offenses. The fact that this has not been more generally attempted in the Southern States shows how the sentiments of the people have grown away from the old slave system. Besides, if a law was passed imposing slavery as a punishment on black culprits it would have to apply to white culprits also; and the possibility of a Negro owning a white slave would seem unpleasant to the ordinary legislator. ("Slavery as a Punishment for Crime" 2)

Hanson's sale was not unique in Kentucky history. For example, a male pauper was sold under the Vagrant Act in Elliott County *circa* May 1871. His wife bought him for 10 cents ("The *Ashland Journal*..." 2).

Tom Ward was sold at public auction in Henderson, Kentucky, on March 20, 1875. Lewis Fisher got him for 20 cents and to show that his heart was in the right place, he also bought Ward a new pair of shoes ("*Henderson* [KY] *Reporter*" 2).

A black man bought a white male vagrant at the Madison County, Kentucky, courthouse in September 1876. The winning bid: five shiny new nickels ("*Richmond* [KY] *Register*" 2).

Three blacks, two notably physically feeble, were sold on the public auction block in Liberty, Virginia, on December 13, 1880; their collective price, $4. They were "vagrants and unable to take care of themselves" ("Great Fall in Flesh" 3).

The *Bowling Green Times* announced in late 1884 that Columbus Ford, "the most incorrigible and irrepressible colored vagrant in the state of Kentucky," would be sold at auction if he did not choose to stay in the county poorhouse ("Kentucky News" 7). Ford's fate is not certain, but in June 1887, Mollie Jackson, a white pauper, was sold into servitude for thirty days at Paducah, McCracken County ("A Woman to be Sold for Vagrancy" 2).

Henry Dodson, described as a "worthless white man," was sentenced in February 1887 to be auctioned in Augusta, Kentucky, for vagrancy. His servitude to the highest bidder was to last seventy-five days ("Henry" 1).

Henry Hart of Russellville, Kentucky, white and about thirty years old, was indicted for vagrancy in early March 1887. He was tried and sentenced to be sold into sixty days of labor at auction. His problem, it seems, was that he was lazy: "Hart is a married man, having a wife and two children, but is constitutionally opposed to work of any kind" ("Fate of a Vagrant" 2). He ended up sold for $1 ("In Kentucky a man..." 12).

On February 9, 1895, the two black women, Sarah Jackson and Bettie Fishback, were sold at public auction at Georgetown, Kentucky; the highest bidders were Henry Jackson and Richard Coleman, who, for a cumulative bid of $3.05, won the labor of the women for a period of six months. Making the matter more intriguing, Jackson and Coleman also were black ("Their Services of Little Value" 3). Northern newspapers protested that the days of slavery had returned to the South. The *Chicago Journal* called the auction "demoralizing" ("The Sale of Vagrants" 4). The *New York Advertiser* said, "Such trafficking in human flesh and blood should be stopped.... [N]o person, black or white, should be permitted to be sold into servitude even for an hour" ("The Sale of Vagrants" 4). The *Atlanta Journal* countered: "A statue in [Kentucky] provides that persons convicted of vagrancy may be sold to the highest bidder to work out their sentences.... This is a very bad law. Still, there no apology or excuse for those Northern newspapers which make an incident in Kentucky the occasion for a wholesale slander of the South" ("The Sale of Vagrants" 4).

The *Georgetown Press* responded to widespread criticism of the sale:

> Some of the philanthropists of the North are unnecessarily disturbed. Letters have been received asking if it is possible that the report is true. There is no need for unnecessary concern on the part of those tender-hearted people. There was neither oppression nor cruelty in the transaction. The women were street-walkers of the lowest class, and had they been consulted would doubtless have preferred to be disposed of in this way to confinement in jail. They had no money with which to pay a fine and wouldn't work if it was offered to them. Some of the good people of the North would do an important favor to suggest some satisfactory plan for dealing with such characters. ("Georgetown's Negro Vagrants" 4)

Several weeks later, in March 1895, another black vagrant, Sol Williams, was sold at the courthouse door in Paris, Kentucky, for $31 for a period of six months' servitude ("Odds and Ends of State News" 4).

The Northern press was offended again when two black vagabonds were auctioned at Lebanon, Kentucky, in late October 1897 ("Matters in Kentucky" 4).

Some Kentucky judges were generous. When an attempt was made to sell a pauper at Maysville in August 1895, Judge Hutchinson ruled that vagrancy is not a crime and refused to allow the auction ("Vagrancy Not a Crime" 1). In a similar incident, Josh Jones was due to be auctioned in Somerset in July 1900; he avoided the punishment only because the judge, T. Z. Morrow, like Judge Hutchinson at Maysville, believed the law was unconstitutional and "out of all proportion to the gravity of the offense" ("The Vagrancy Law" 4).

On the other hand, Deputy Sheriff M. H. Williams allowed the auction of a white hobo, Lawrence Peak, at the Elizabethtown courthouse in Hardin County on August 3, 1896. His purchaser, John Cecil, got six months' worth of work out of Peak for $12.75 ("A Vagrant Sold" 5).

Arch Hays, a farmer who lived near Taylorsville, Spencer County, purchased at auction the services of a black vagrant, Sy Lewis, for nine months for only $2 around August 6, 1901 ("Taylorsville Vagrant Sold..." 1).

On September 6, 1902, Shelbyville, Kentucky's Sheriff R. Walter Briggs auctioned off a Fisher Million, described as a "worthless Negro" who "enjoys the distinction of never having worked a day in his life." The winner was to get a year's labor from Million. Perhaps the residents were uncharitable with Million since he had infected the town with smallpox in 1900, costing the city several thousand dollars in health care costs ("Negro Vagrant Will Be Offered for Sale..." 1). The winning bid, $4, was made by well-respected black farmer David Murphy, who told Million that he would be treated well and would have plenty to eat and wear, but also vowed that he would make the hobo work even if he had to apply a whip. "Murphy afterward said he would have bid as high as $20 on the vagrant Negro. He said he bought him from a purely speculative standpoint, intending to make him work, and that no sentiment whatever governed him in making his strange purchase." An eyewitness reported, "Many Negroes attended the sale, and the fact that the vagrant was purchased by one of their color completely changed sentiment among them, and instead of mutterings which would have been the case had he been bought by a white man, the result meets with their hearty approval" ("Negro Farmer Purchases a Black Brother..." 1). A few weeks later, Murphy received a threatening letter from a black organization at Hampden, Virginia ("Shelbyville" 8).

On November 28, 1902, three black paupers—two women, Belle Griffin and Emma Reed, and a man named Charles Anderson—were sold at auction in Lancaster, Kentucky. Anderson's services went for $7, while Griffin and Reed brought $5 apiece. Anderson and Griffin were sold into servitude for one year, but Reed got three years ("Two Negro Women Sell" 1).

Bruce Marcum, white, a "young, robust, and able-bodied man about twenty-seven years of age," was sold at public auction by the Breathitt County, Kentucky's Sheriff Berry Turner on April 8, 1903. Turner "performed the duty with all the skill of a professional auctioneer, calling attention to the health and physical qualities of the young man, and impressing upon the crowd the value of the young man's labor." The winning bid for six months of Marcum's servitude was $6.50, placed by William Griffith. Marcum was the nephew of attorney and

United States Commissioner J. B. Marcum of Jackson, but his family connections did not save him from the auction block ("Young White Man Sold for Vagrancy" 6).

Dock Aubury of Meeting Creek, Hardin County, Kentucky, was another white male who got purchased at auction. The *Elizabethtown News* described him as being "a strong, able-bodied man without means of support and too lazy to work." The paper added, "The town and county would be much benefited if more of such prosecutions were made against the worthless lot of loafers that can be found on the streets here at any time" ("Will Sell White Man" 4). Aubury had recently got married and made the mistake of moving in with the bride's family and then refusing to work. When the in-laws got sick of his mooching, they instigated proceedings to have him tried as a vagrant. On December 3, 1906, blacksmith J. J. Johnson of Rineyville bought Aubury for only $1 before a large and sarcastic crowd. This means that Johnson got Aubury's services for a year at a cost of less than half a cent per day ("Human Being's Price" 2). However, Aubury's servitude did not last long. On December 9, the judge ruled that the jury which convicted him had been improperly instructed and the grateful pauper was set free ("Sets Aside Sale of White Man" 1).

Lest anyone think post-war auctioning of people was strictly a Kentucky phenomenon, there are cases in other states after the war. A white female pauper went to the highest bidder at the Wirt County, West Virginia, courthouse in January 1869 ("A white female pauper..." 2). In July of the same year, a black male vagrant was sold at Glasgow, Missouri, for $14 ("A Negro man was sold at auction..." 2.).

In early January 1875, Charles Rogers, "a white man who has no visible means of support," was sold at auction for a sixty-day period of involuntary servitude by order of the mayor of Petersburg, Virginia. He was sold on a stand at the courthouse, which must have brought back memories of slave auctions. The local paper remarked, "We do not know whether to congratulate or condole with the man who will get him" ("*Petersburg* [VA] *Index*" 2).

A man in Evansville, Indiana, was sold for 20 cents in March 1875 ("An Evansville man..." 3).

Two white pauper women, Mollie Mitchell and Ida Jones, were sold at the courthouse door at Springfield, Missouri, in early August 1875. Despite the auctioneer's praising her fine qualities, the glum Mollie didn't receive a single bid, which visibly annoyed her. On the other hand, Ida, "with agile step and smiling face," was sold for 5 cents. Even so, her purchaser had to borrow the nickel from a bystander. Then the buyer was given Mollie as well in a sort of BOGO sale. "This is a serious subject," said the local paper. "It is almost incredible that such things could be in this enlightened land of churches and benevolent societies" ("Two White Women Sold..." 3).

On April 5, 1876, "decent, respectable, but poor unfortunate [white] females" and "a poor, blind white man" in the local paper's words, were sold to black purchasers in Trenton, North Carolina ("Magnolia [N.C.]" 2).

A hobo auction occurred in Fayette, Missouri, on March 28, 1892 ("Negroes Sold at Auction" 1); Elmira Quick, age seventy-seven, was put on the auction block by overseers of the poor in Lackawaxen Township, Pennsylvania, in January 1899, and put a winning bid on herself ("A Pauper Bids Herself In" 4).

The clause allowing sale of humans as punishment for crime remains in the Thirteenth Amendment—theoretically valid, though not practically.

20
Belated Discoveries

In 1863 Henry J. Raymond of the *New York Times* received a government notice reading, "Your brother's corpse is at Belle Plaine." Raymond took off for that city with a heavy heart to retrieve his soldier brother's body and provide it with dignified services. Raymond arrived to find him perfectly alive and healthy. An investigation revealed that the dispatch's intended message had been "Your brother's corps is at Belle Plaine." "The circumstance is very funny," said a news report ("Hon. Henry J. Raymond..." 1).

A nineteen-year-old woman from Brooklyn—the earliest press reports about her exploits, from February 1864, identified her only as Emily and noted that she lived on Willoughby Street—was quite taken with the idea in 1863 that she was destined to be a modern Joan of Arc. She was so determined to enlist that her alarmed parents sent her to live with relatives in Ann Arbor, Michigan. They confined her to an apartment, but she escaped, cut her hair short, and successfully enlisted in Detroit in the Army of the Cumberland.

She became a drummer and survived several battles in Kentucky, but her disguise came to an end when she was mortally wounded by a Minié ball in her left side at Lookout Mountain, Tennessee, on November 24, 1863. She survived long enough to write a poignant letter to her father: "Forgive your dying daughter; I have but a few moments to live. My native soil drinks my blood. I expected to deliver my country, but the fates would not have it so. I am content to die. Pray, Pa, forgive me. Tell Ma to kiss my daguerreotype. P.S. Give my gold watch to little Eph." Eph was her youngest brother. Emily was buried in the field as befitting the soldier she truly was ("Romantic History and Death" 4; "A Romantic Incident" 1).

Another woman in disguise was discovered in 1934 when Mancil Milligan tended his garden at his home near Tennessee's Shiloh National Military Park and uncovered the resting place of nine long-forgotten Union soldiers. Forensics experts who examined the skeletons said one was that of a woman who still bore a Minié ball near her ribs (Garrison *More Civil War* 98). The grave yielded bits of uniforms but no feminine apparel, leading to the conclusion that she had been disguised as a soldier. The nine skeletons were buried in the Shiloh national cemetery in Section R, grave 3633.

Mr. Holly lived in an isolated section of Hogback Mountain, near Greenville, South Carolina, with his slave Calvin Garmany. Holly refused to allow him to visit relatives.

With good cause: he didn't want Garmany to know that slavery had ended in 1865, twenty-two years before. The illegally held slave was rescued by his brother in February 1887 ("Just Learned of Negro Emancipation" 2).

In a similar case, Joseph Hickman of Cooper County, Missouri, purchased a female slave at the beginning of the war and would not permit her to leave the farm. After he died in December 1889, she escaped to Boonville, where she learned that she legally had been free for a long time. She sued Hickman's estate for $1,400 in wages, of which the Probate Court allowed $700 ("American Slavery" 2).

On August 23, 1893, Marina Estinoz, a twenty-six-year-old so-called "octoroon" (a person having one-eighth black ancestry) from Cuba, discovered for the first time that slavery had ended and that her mistress Isabella Estinoz had no right to hold her. Marina hastily filed suit against Isabella for $2,500 for having not let her in on this elementary fact. This occurred not in the Deep South but in Brooklyn, New York ("Slave Just Freed" 4).

A man named Landers in Jacktown, Pennsylvania, acquired a slave girl at the beginning of the war. He didn't inform her of her liberty at the war's end, and never told her she was living in a free state to begin with. He kept her illiterate so she'd never find out. He swapped her for a horse and whisky in September 1875, when she was fifteen years old, and then authorities discovered his secret ("Pennsylvania as a Slave State" 1).

In June 1869, a man emerged from Florida's Everglades with two slaves to sell. Not only did he not know slavery had ended, he was not even aware there had been a war ("Rip Van Winkle" 3). Perhaps when he first ventured into town, he said something like "Hey, did anything happen while I was away?"

Edward Brown of Pitt County, North Carolina, was a draft dodger. To accomplish this end, in 1863 he hid deep in the backwoods and became a hermit. He remained undetected until June 1871, when someone in the forest encountered him clad only in homemade clothes made of animal skins. Brown insisted to his finder that he would not join the army. Imagine his surprise when told the war had ended six years before, and that both his parents died in 1870. Having not conversed with a human being in eight years, Brown had a great deal of trouble articulating his speech, except for swear words. Those he remembered ("The New Bern *Republican*..." 2). This is the story as related by a contemporary New Bern paper.

During the Third Battle of Winchester, Virginia, on September 19, 1864, a unionist citizen asked Major Parsons, United States Provost Marshal, if he would supply a guard to watch over his property. A man whom press reports call John W. from the 2nd New York Cavalry was assigned the job, with orders "to remain until he was relieved by proper authority." He followed orders well—arguably, too well. He was never relieved of his duty and remained at his post nearly three years after the war ended. It was reported in March 1868 that he was finally about to be relieved and would receive proper financial remuneration ("A Remarkable Story" 1).

In November 1911, A. N. Lent of Superior, Wisconsin, formerly first lieutenant in the 92nd Indiana Volunteers, claimed that he never had been officially mustered out of the service at the war's end and therefore technically had been in active service for nearly fifty years. He informed the War Department that the government owed him $90,000 worth of back salary, not including interest ("Peculiar Claim Made..." 4). What happened next? I do not know, but strongly suspect it did not end well for the creative Mr. Lent.

Private William Newby of Company D, 4th Regiment, Illinois Volunteers, was reported killed in action at Shiloh in April 1862. But he wasn't. Instead, he received a head wound that affected his mental processes. Considered harmlessly insane, he was taken prisoner by the Confederates and confined at Belle Isle, and later transferred to Andersonville. After release from that prison camp, Newby wandered the South, spending time in various poorhouses. An uncle finally recognized him—but didn't tell anyone else in the family—and Newby lived with him in Key West until the uncle died in 1869. Then he took to the wandering life again.

In Shreveport a group of sympathetic blacks collected money and bought him fare on a Cincinnati-bound steamboat. When the vessel docked briefly in Shawneetown, Illinois, a ship official called out the city's name. A chord struck in Newby's brain; the city sounded familiar to him for some reason. He got off the boat to satisfy his curiosity and walked to Kankakee, then McLean. Finally, in 1891, he made it to White County, Illinois, his original home. While there, two of his old regimental comrades fortuitously recognized him. They had not seen him in twenty-nine years. His putative widow was sent for. She recognized him, as did many friends and family members.

His wife had been collecting a widow's pension since 1862. The payments stopped when Newby turned up alive. He applied for a pension of his own, but since he had been assumed dead, he never was officially discharged. The pension was granted, but only after the secretary of war pronounced him a living veteran and no longer on active duty ("A Wanderer for Years" 4).

Several boys were coon hunting 3 miles north of Sandersville, Georgia, near the end of September 1893. They saw a campfire and investigated. They found an old man, a stranger to them, digging at a large boulder near a spring and muttering to himself. Suddenly, perhaps overcome by his exertions, he clutched his throat and died. The hunters saw all they wanted to and hurried home to tell the authorities.

Coroner Lowe came to the scene to inspect the body. He found papers revealing the man's identity as Eugene Starr of Holyoke, Massachusetts, and his reason for being so far from home. During the Civil War, two of General Sherman's men became detached from their comrades and wandered the Georgia countryside until one—Frederick Starr, a member of Company G, 11th Massachusetts Regiment, and the dead man's son—got sick and died near Sandersville. Starr's friend buried him on the north side of the boulder. The surviving soldier continued drifting without informing Starr's family and eventually settled in California. Many years later, just before his death, he wrote an account of his friend's burial and ordered that it be sent to Frederick Starr's relatives.

It was evident to the coroner that Eugene Starr had died while searching for his son's last resting place. But was the story of the burial true? Close inspection showed that the letters "U. S." were faintly carved in the boulder. Coroner Lowe set a crew digging, and beneath a thin layer of rocks they found a skeleton dressed in a rotted Federal uniform. To make sure, Lowe sent a telegram to the mayor of Holyoke and was informed that Eugene Starr had in fact disappeared weeks before, and that he had brooded for years over the unknown fate of his only son, a Union soldier who had been last seen in Georgia. The elderly Starr had not the money to pay for a train ride, and to find his son's body he must have walked from Massachusetts to Georgia.

The folks in Sandersville made a proper grave for the long-lost Frederick Starr and a coffin large enough to hold both father and son ("An Old Father's Love" 2).

One day late in May, twenty-five years after the Civil War ended, some boys fishing on the river near Wayne City, Missouri, found a long-forgotten cave. They explored it, but when it became too narrow, they were afraid to venture farther. Word of the cave got out, and within days a party of more adventurous explorers were crawling the narrow passageway.

After 50 feet, the passage opened into a chamber containing a pile of muskets, their rotten stocks long since eaten by worms; a haversack; a memorandum book dated April 7, 1863; and the apparent former owner of these things, a human skeleton that had been scattered by an animal. The first entry in the book read, "We were shelled by the Federals from up the river in a gunboat."

The second entry: "We had a skirmish with the Federals at the landing. After a strong fight they were beaten off."

The next several pages consisted of columns of numbers, and handwritten extracts from letters and books which the soldier appeared to have recounted from memory.

The final entry: "I am wounded in the left side and the rest of the boys were run off. Jim has gone for a doctor, but he can't save—" ("Skeleton in a Cave" 2).

Sometime in the autumn of 1863, four men disappeared without a trace from the vicinity of Colliers, West Virginia: John Ewing, Ben Ayers, Tom Ackleson, and Joe Obney. The mystery stood until February 1896, when David Snyder explored an abandoned coal mine a mile east of town. The mine had caved in, and when Snyder removed boulders, he found four skeletons, one of which was sitting against a ledge. The mine also yielded a flask containing a note written in pencil:

> November 2, 1863.—Should this ever reach the outside world let it be known that we [naming the four missing men] are prisoners here, owing to the caving in of the mine. We are deserters, and were in hiding here when the mine caved in. Food and water all gone. We are doomed, as no one outside is aware of our whereabouts. This is about the eighth day of our imprisonment.
>
> November 4—John Ewing and Tom Ackleson have just killed Ben Ayers and are eating him. I have already eaten my boot leg. The water in the mine is terrible. Our oil is getting scarce, air becoming foul. I only know the day of the month by my watch.
>
> November 6—Ewing has just killed Ackleson. Cut off one of his feet and is eating it, and dancing around and flourishing his dirk knife like a maniac.
>
> November 7—I am now alone with the dead. I had to kill Ewing in self-defense. I have just eaten my other boot leg. Am sleepy. Good bye. I inclose [*sic*] this note in this flask to preserve it if possible, so that if ever found our sad fate will be known. JOSEPH OBNEY.

Residents remembered the four men and had long assumed they were killed in battle. None of the four had living relatives, and an undertaker gave them a charitable burial ("A Diary of Horror" 1).

21
Love and War

At the turn of the twentieth century, visitors to the John Bell farm near Hodgenville, Kentucky, could see a beech tree, on which the name James Pitman was carved. He was a tall, handsome, mustached Confederate soldier in Bragg's army who took ill while camping nearby. He was carried unconscious to Bell's house, where he died after waking just long enough to say, "Tell Nellie that I wanted to see her before I died." He had no papers to provide further clues as to his hometown or the identity of Nellie. All that was known about him were his name and that he hailed from Tennessee. Bell buried Pitman in a grove of trees. Perhaps Nellie spent the rest of her life wondering what happened to her missing soldier ("Soldier's Lone Grave" 5).

Slave Levi was owned by Mr. Sparks of Morgan County, Georgia, *circa* 1840. In the same county, Dr. E. E. Jones owned Aggie, a mulatto girl. Levi met Aggie often at corn shuckings and dances and, as their relationship became more serious, he got passes from Mr. Sparks to visit her on Saturday nights. Levi and Aggie married in 1843.

But in 1844 Sparks moved to Polk County and took his slaves with him. Levi was brokenhearted by the enforced separation. Around 1850, convinced he would never see his Aggie again, he married for a second time. Over time, Aggie too came to think her life with Levi was over and married another man, raising a large family with him.

Then came the Civil War, the collapse of the Confederacy, and freedom for the slaves. Levi made discreet inquiries and found that Aggie was still alive but married. In 1874, her second husband died, but Levi was still married to his second wife. After she passed away in 1882, both Levi and Aggie were single again. After a few months they remarried, picking up where they had left off forty years before. "Their love is young again," remarked a journalist. As of January 1884, the couple lived happily in Cedartown Valley near Rome. "Everybody in the neighborhood has heard the sad story," said the reporter, "and they are recipients of many kindnesses" ("A Romance of Slavery Days" 4).

In 1839, slave David Walke was sold away from his home in Norfolk, Virginia, to New Orleans, leaving behind his wife, Nancy Gibbs. In 1870, Walke returned to Norfolk and found that Gibbs was alive, well, and unmarried. He acquired a marriage license, and the next day he remarried Gibbs. He was eighty-three and she was seventy-four. "Such constancy and indubitable evidence of affection, outliving time and absence, deserve notice," said the local paper ("The *Norfolk Virginian* relates…" 2).

Philip Carr of Ohio joined the army after Lincoln's second call for volunteers in 1862, leaving behind his wife of a year and his baby daughter. He wrote home often but his letters abruptly ceased after several months because Confederate guerrillas had confiscated the Federals' mail. Mrs. Carr concluded that her husband had deserted her. She got a divorce, remarried, and moved East. When Carr returned home, he learned that his wife had divorced him and vacated. He remarried too, perhaps out of pique.

Decades later, after their respective spouses were dead, Carr revisited his boyhood home and saw his first wife, also on a visit. He explained that his letters home had been stolen; she gave her side of it; they gazed into each other's eyes and their hearts' dormant hearths were rekindled. The upshot is that they remarried in August 1910 and settled in Kenton. The elderly couple said "the tragedy of errors had been made up to them by their happiness now" ("Happy Ending to Shattered Romance" 3).

It was the unpleasant duty of the New Orleans coroner, in November 1861, to hold an inquest on a young woman not even out of her teen years, "belonging to a high and distinguished family," who had committed suicide. Her husband of two years left for the war, and one night she dreamed of his death in battle. She believed so strongly in the vision that she drank morphine without checking out the facts first. She didn't even relate her plan to friends or family members, who might have talked her out of it ("Melancholy Suicide" 4).

Just as Carrie De Witt was about to have been married back in 1861, her boyfriend went off to war and never returned. She never found out what happened to him and remained unmarried. She died in Friona, Texas, on April 11, 1931, and was buried in the vintage wedding dress she never got to wear in life ("Death Brings End to Vigil of Love" 10).

A young Mississippian died at the Battle of the Wilderness. Just before burial, a letter from his sweetheart arrived. A thoughtful minister placed it on the dead soldier's chest, remarking, "Bury it with him. He will see it when he wakes" ("We remember..." 4).

Bibliography

Chapter 1

"Another Slave Case," *Louisville Courier*, August 17, 1852, 3
"Arrested on a Felony Warrant," *Louisville Courier*, May 4, 1861, 4
Borries, F., "Sold at Auction by Her Father," *Louisville Courier-Journal*, February 27, 1938, magazine, 1
"C-J Feature Gets Mrs. Wickliffe on Ripley Program," *Louisville Courier-Journal*, March 30, 1938, I, 2
"Cupidity Versus Cupid," *Louisville Courier*, March 17, 1860, 1
"A curious case is reported from Missouri…" *Louisville Journal*, July 4, 1867, 1
"In Jail," *Louisville Courier*, December 28, 1860, 1
"Inquest No. 248," *Louisville Courier*, December 27, 1860, 1
"Interesting to Slaveholders," *Louisville Courier*, April 9, 1858, 1
"John, a slave…" *Louisville Courier*, January 1, 1861, 1
"Julius Hawkins," *Louisville Journal*, March 30, 1849, 2
"The Lucky Prize Freedom," *Louisville Courier*, April 9, 1857, 3
"Murder for Ten Cents," *Louisville Courier*, December 27, 1860, 1
"The Negro Case," *Louisville Courier*, November 11, 1859, 1
"[Negro] in Luck," *Louisville Courier*, April 8, 1857, 3
"Negro Marriages," *Louisville Journal*, March 5, 1868, 1
"The Negro Martin…" *Louisville Courier*, August 16, 1852, 3
"Novel Decision," *Louisville Journal*, November 25, 1842, 3
"A Novel Trial," *Louisville Courier*, November 15, 1851, 3
"Police Court," *Louisville Courier*, November 17, 1851, 2
"Police Court," *Louisville Courier*, August 16, 1852, 3
"Police Court," *Louisville Courier*, August 17, 1852, 3
"Reese Wins His Wife and Children," *Louisville Courier*, June 16, 1859, 1
"Sale of an Insane Negro," *Louisville Courier*, November 10, 1859, 1
"Selling a Crazy Negro," *Louisville Courier*, November 9, 1859, 1
"Simon Porter…" *Louisville Courier*, October 6, 1848, 1
"Singular Sale of Slaves," *Louisville Courier*, March 12, 1852, 2
"The slave John…" *Louisville Courier*, January 1, 1861, 1
"Two slaves employed…" *Louisville Courier*, September 5, 1854, 3
"A slave, convicted of killing…" *Louisville Journal*, December 4, 1845, 2
"A White Woman Released from Slavery," *Louisville Courier*, November 6, 1851, 3
"Woman, Sold as Baby, Succumbs," *Louisville Courier-Journal*, March 22, 1939, I, 14

Chapter 2

Bell, W. S., *The Camel Regiment: A History of the Bloody 43rd Mississippi Volunteer Infantry 1862–65* (Gretna, LA.: Pelican Publishing Co., 2017)
"A Brave Bird..." *Louisville Journal*, July 14, 1864, 3
"Buried with Wings," *Louisville Courier-Journal*, November 28, 1909, IV, 3
"A correspondent states..." *Louisville Journal*, April 10, 1866, 4
"A dead mule..." *Louisville Journal*, June 1, 1864, 3
"Denies Quantrill is Still Living," *Louisville Courier-Journal*, August 25, 1907, I, 4
"Eugenia Philips," *History of American Women*. January 2007, www.womenhistoryblog.com/2007/01/eugenia-phillips.html
Garrison, W., *Civil War Curiosities* (Nashville: Rutledge Hill Press, 1994); *More Civil War Curiosities* (Nashville: Rutledge Hill Press, 1995)
"Gen. W.K. Kimball..." *Louisville Courier-Journal*, September 11, 1875, 3
George, J. G., "Rebel Occupancy of Richmond, Ky," *Louisville Journal*, November 8, 1862, 3
"Guerrilla Quantrell [*sic*] in Washington," *Louisville Journal*, March 24, 1866, 4
"The horrid wretch Quantrell [*sic*]..." *Louisville Journal*, December 2, 1865, 2
"Identification of Guerrilla Quantrell [*sic*]," *Louisville Journal*, March 15, 1866, 4
"It is rumored..." *Louisville Journal*, October 17, 1862, 3
"MCZ Herpetology R-570," Museum of Comparative Zoology, Harvard, *mczbase*, 2024, mczbase.mcz.harvard.edu/guid/MCZ:Herp:R-570
"The Mockingbird of Resaca," *Louisville Journal*, July 12, 1864, 3
"Not One Hurt..." *Louisville Courier-Journal*, December 26, 1909, I, 4
"Quantrill's Body Rests in Ohio..." *Louisville Courier-Journal*, April 12, 1922, 8
"Quantrell [*sic*], the Missouri guerrilla..." *Louisville Journal*, March 13, 1866, 2
"Richmond Battle at Big Hill," *Louisville Journal*, October 17, 1862, 3
"The Rumored Fight at Big Hill," *Louisville Journal*, October 18, 1862, 1
"Secret Testimony," *Louisville Journal*, June 16, 1865, 1
"Seventy-Five Thousand Tons of Human Blood," *Louisville Journal*, August 11, 1864, 1
"A Singular Spectacle in Battle," *Louisville Journal*, July 4, 1863, 1
"Such of the hogs as are left..." *Louisville Journal*, October 24, 1862, 2
"A War Story about John Morgan..." *Louisville Courier-Journal*, October 30, 1892, 4
"A Washington dispatch..." *Louisville Journal*, April 2, 1866, 3
"We are informed by a correspondent..." *Louisville Journal*, October 20, 1862, 3
"Woman in a Soldier Cemetery," *Louisville Courier-Journal*, January 9, 1898, I, 7

Chapter 3

"A Bullet in His Neck," *Louisville Courier-Journal*, March 25, 1894, 7
"The *Clinton* [LA] *Patriot* describes..." *Louisville Courier-Journal*, August 19, 1871, 2
"Coughing Up a Bullet," *Louisville Courier-Journal*, May 24, 1881, 1
"A Curious Experience," *Louisville Courier-Journal*, August 5, 1891, 4
"A Curious Set of Wounds," *Louisville Courier*, July 8, 1862, 3
"The *Franklin*..." *Louisville Courier-Journal* October 31, 1870, 2
Garrison, W., *Civil War Curiosities* (Nashville: Rutledge Hill Press, 1994); *More Civil War Curiosities* (Nashville: Rutledge Hill Press, 1995)
"A Last Will and Testament," *Louisville Courier*, May 28, 1864, 1
"A late New Orleans paper says..." *Louisville Journal*, May 14, 1864, 4

"A lieutenant at the late battle..." *Louisville Journal*, March 14, 1864, 4
"Major Moderwell..." *Louisville Courier-Journal*. March 20, 1872, 3
"A Man Carries a Bull Run Bullet..." *Louisville Courier*, March 16, 1867, 1
"A Miraculous Escape," *Louisville Journal*, August 18, 1864, 1
"*Nashville Banner*," *Louisville Courier-Journal*, April 26, 1875, 2
"An 'Off-Hand' Joke," *Louisville Courier*, June 1, 1864, 1
"A Remarkable Case," *Louisville Journal*, May 23, 1864, 3
"Richard H. Scott..." *Louisville Courier-Journal*, January 8, 1870, 2
"Savannah..." *Louisville Courier-Journal*, October 23, 1873, 2
"A Singular Case," *Louisville Courier-Journal*, June 15, 1870 (daily edition), 4
"A Strange Account of the Effect..." *Louisville Journal*, February 12, 1867, 3
"The Tenacity of Life," *Louisville Courier*, May 22, 1867, 3
"A Tribute to Gallantry," *Louisville Journal*, September 13, 1866, 1
"A Volunteer Shave," *Louisville Courier*, March 1, 1864, 4
"Wounded," *Louisville Courier*, November 11, 1863, 1
"The Yankee Passion Strong in Death," *Louisville Courier*, January 13, 1865, 4

Chapter 4

"Another Guerrilla to Be Hung Tomorrow," *Louisville Journal*, April 18, 1865, 3
"Bruce's Brigade ... Military Execution," *Louisville Journal*, February 7, 1862, 2
"By Order of Court-Martial," *Louisville Courier-Journal*, January 6, 1882, 6
"Captain Green..." *Louisville Journal*, February 28, 1862, 3
"Court-Martial for Murder," *Louisville Journal*, February 4, 1862, 3
"Died in Prison," *Louisville Journal*, June 25, 1864, 3
"The editors of the *Journal* sincerely and deeply regret..." *Louisville Journal*, April 21, 1865, 2
"Execution at Memphis," *Louisville Journal*, May 5, 1864, 1
"Execution of a Rebel Spy," *Louisville Journal*, December 15, 1863, 1
"Execution of Dodd at Knoxville," *Louisville Journal*, February 4, 1864, 4
"Execution of J. J. Straney," *Louisville Journal*, April 28, 1865, 3
"Execution of Joseph Minix," *Louisville Journal*, June 22, 1863, 1
"Execution of Nathaniel Marks," *Louisville Journal*, January 21, 1865, 3
"Homicide Near Bardstown," *Louisville Journal*, January 25, 1862, 3
"John T. Bishop..." *Louisville Journal*, August 24, 1865, 3
"Kennedy's Execution," *New York Times*, March 27, 1865, 8
"A Military Execution," *Louisville Courier-Journal*, November 16, 1890, 20
"Military Execution," *Louisville Journal*, February 11, 1862, 2
"Mrs. C.A. Underwood..." *Louisville Courier-Journal*, June 15, 1874, 2
"Robert Cobb Kennedy..." *Louisville Journal*, March 26, 1865, 3
"Sentenced to Be Shot," *Louisville Journal*, March 28, 1864, 1
"A singular tragedy..." *Louisville Courier-Journal*, April 12, 1874, 2
"Six Unhallowed Graves," *Nashville Banner*, May 29, 1882, 2
"A Soldier's Lone Grave," *Louisville Courier-Journal*, June 24, 1900, II, 4
Stevens, L. T., *History of Cape New County, N.J.* (Cape May: Lewis Stevens, 1897)
"To Be Hung," *Louisville Journal*, January 20, 1865, 3
"To the editors..." *Louisville Journal*, February 20, 1864, 1
"While Thinking of J. Wilkes Booth..." *Louisville Journal*, April 19, 1865, 3

CHAPTER 5

"An Affectionate Son," *Louisville Journal*, August 21, 1863, 1
"All for Love," *Louisville Courier*, November 18, 1861, 1
"At Hartford, a colored hotel waiter..." *Louisville Journal*, August 11, 1863, 1
"At Terre Haute..." *Louisville Journal*, July 1, 1863, 1
"At Windsor, Canada..." *Louisville Journal*, March 21, 1863, 1
"Cincinnati: In Boone County..." *Louisville Journal*, June 20, 1863, 1
"Conscription vs. Matrimony," *Louisville Journal*, April 25, 1863, 1
"Cowardly Self-Mutilation," *Louisville Journal*, August 20, 1862, 3
"Draft Dodgers in Difficulty," *Louisville Journal*, August 13, 1862, 3
"A Drafting Dodge," *Louisville Journal*, August 21, 1862, 1
"An 'Exemption' Trick," *Louisville Journal*, July 29, 1863, 1
"A Fool: John Trulock..." *Louisville Journal*, November 16, 1864, 3
Garrison, W., *More Civil War Curiosities* (Nashville: Rutledge Hill Press, 1995)
"A gay deserter..." *Louisville Journal*, September 4, 1863, 3
"Interesting Case: A Good Master," *Louisville Journal*, October 15, 1864, 3
"It is believed there are 15,000..." *Louisville Journal*, April 8, 1864, 4
"It is reported in an Ohio paper..." *Louisville Journal*, August 22, 1863, 1
"Loud Calls for Substitutes," *Louisville Journal*, March 6, 1862, 4
"Maimed Himself," *Louisville Journal*, October 17, 1862, 3
"A man at Amesbury, Mass..." *Louisville Journal*, June 1, 1864, 3
"Matrimony has proved a good speculation..." *Louisville Journal*, April 15, 1863, 1
"Men are marrying at the East..." *Louisville Journal*, April 25, 1863, 1
"The Michigan gentleman..." *Louisville Journal*, September 1, 1862, 2
"Milwaukee: In justice..." *Louisville Journal*, November 17, 1862, 3
"A Negro in Washington..." *Louisville Journal*, September 1, 1863, 1
"A New Jersey millionaire..." *Louisville Journal*, August 23, 1862, 2
"The notice of the bill to repeal..." *Louisville Journal*, December 9, 1863, 1
"Persons without front teeth..." *Louisville Journal*, September 10, 1862, 2
"Profitable Speculation," *Louisville Journal*, December 10, 1862, 1
"A rebel agent has been at work..." *Louisville Journal*, April 14, 1862, 2
"Refugees from Northern Despotism," *Louisville Courier*, December 2, 1861, 4
"The *St. Catharines* [Canada] *Journal*..." *Louisville Journal*, April 21, 1863, 2
"The sentiment of the Senate respecting the $300 exemption..." *Louisville Journal*, December 24, 1863, 1
"Shameful," *Louisville Journal*, August 7, 1862, 1
"Some indications of resistance to the draft..." *Louisville Journal*, August 4, 1863, 1
"A Substitute Runs Away..." *Louisville Journal*, October 6, 1864, 4
"Those who have escaped to Canada..." *Louisville Journal*, October 5, 1864, 1
"A thousand dollars is the price..." *Louisville Journal*, April 25, 1862, 2
"Thousands of the persons drafted..." *Louisville Journal*, January 13, 1862, 2
"The Three Hundred Dollars Exemption," *Louisville Journal*, July 7, 1863, 1
"A volunteer in the Second Brigade..." *Louisville Courier*, June 15, 1861, 4
"The War Department has definitely concluded..." *Louisville Journal*, July 9, 1863, 3
"The Women the Cause of the Resistance..." *Louisville Journal*, November 17, 1862, 1
"Working Both Ways," *Louisville Journal*, May 2, 1864, 1

Chapter 6

"Dead Rebel Taken for a Back-Log," *Louisville Journal*, December 8, 1864, 3
"The following inscription…" *Louisville Courier-Journal*, August 1, 1870, 2
Garrison, W., *Civil War Curiosities* (Nashville: Rutledge Hill Press, 1994)
"Gen. Sherman's 'bummers'…" *Louisville Journal*, May 20, 1865, 3
"Gone to the Front," *Louisville Courier-Journal*, September 5, 1886, 5
"In Providence last week…" *Louisville Journal*, July 18, 1863, 3
"The last slave sold in the Confederacy…" *Louisville Courier-Journal*, June 30, 1879, 2
"Libby prison…" *Louisville Journal*, January 18, 1866, 1
"Manassas…" *Louisville Journal*, August 24, 1868, 2
Morris, Jr., R., *Ambrose Bierce: Alone in Bad Company* (NY and Oxford: Oxford University Press, 1995)
"Never Was Free Before," *Louisville Courier-Journal*, December 24, 1895, 5
"The people of North Carolina…" *Louisville Journal*, November 13, 1866, 1
"Sedgwick's Death," *Indianapolis Sentinel*, June 14, 1885, 11
"A Strange Story, If True," *Louisville Journal*, November 15, 1864, 3
"The Suicide at Camp Carrington," *Louisville Journal*, March 24, 1865, 1
"The Twin Brothers," *Louisville Journal*, April 17, 1866, 4

Chapter 7

"All Over the South," *Louisville Courier-Journal*, September 26, 1882, 4
Andrews, M. P., *Virginia, the Old Dominion* (Richmond, VA, Dietz Press, 1949)
Aurandt, P., *Destiny* (New York: Bantam, 1984)
Bruce, P. A., *Institutional History of Virginia in the Seventeenth Century, Volume 2* (New York: G. P. Putnam's Sons, 1910)
"The Council of the Cherokees…" *Louisville Journal*, December 24, 1850, 3
"Death of a Remarkable Negro," *Louisville Courier-Journal*, June 6, 1868, 1.
"Emancipation Board Report in 1862 is Studied by the Rambler," Washington, D.C., *Evening Star*, June 12, 1927, 74
"Holding Slaves," *Louisville Courier*, March 29, 1858, 1
"In Abolitionist Indiana," *Louisville Courier-Journal*, March 8, 1891, 5
Jordan, Jr., E. L., "Different Drummers: Black Virginians as Confederate Loyalists," in *Black Southerners in Gray: Essays in Afro-Americans in Confederate Armies*, ed. Richard Rollins, *Journal of Confederate History Studies, Vol. XI* (Murfreesboro, TN: Southern Heritage Press, 1994)
Koger, L., *Black Slaveowners: Free Black Slave Masters in South Carolina, 1790–1860* (Jefferson, N.C.: McFarland, 1985)
"Many Negroes Owned Slaves…" *Charleston News and Courier*. Reprinted in *Louisville Courier-Journal,* June 4, 1907, 9
Mapp, Jr., A. J., *The Virginia Experiment* (Lanham, MD: Hamilton Press, 1957, 1985)
McCarthy, J., "About the Chief Seattle Speech," *Stanford*, October 6, 2003, jmc.stanford.edu/commentary/progress/fake.html
McManus, E. J., *Black Bondage in the North* (Syracuse: Syracuse University Press, 1973)
McQueen, K., *Weird Wild West* (Bloomington: University of Indiana Press, 2019)
"A Negro Slaveholder," *Louisville Courier-Journal,* October 6, 1891, 2
"Negroes Among the Indians," *Pittsburgh Gazette*, September 13, 1875, 1
"Negroes in the Creek Nation," *Louisville Courier-Journal*, February 21, 1901, 3

"Negroes Who Owned Negro Slaves," *Nashville Union*, reprinted in *St. Louis Globe Democrat*, September 3, 1886, 4
Olmsted, F. L., *Journey in the Seaboard Slave States* (New York: Negro Universities Press, 1968. Reprint of 1856 edition)
Potter, G., "Catholicism in the Old South," Catholicism.org, May 16, 2005, catholicism.org/catholicism-south.html
Rollins, R., "Black Southerners in Gray," in *Black Southerners in Gray: Essays in Afro Americans in Confederate Armies*, ed. Richard Rollins, *Journal of Confederate History Studies, Vol. XI* (Murfreesboro, TN: Southern Heritage Press, 1994)
Schweninger, L., "Prosperous Blacks in the South, 1790–1880," *American Historical Review*, February 1990, 31-56
"A Slave State in Embryo," *Louisville Journal*, December 2, 1850, 2
"Slavery in Florida," *Louisville Courier-Journal,* January 5, 1890, 6
"Slavery Not Extinct," *Philadelphia Press,* May 15, 1883, 5
"A splendid sugar plantation..." *Louisville Courier*, June 22, 1858, 1
Starkey, M. L., *The Cherokee Nation* (New York: Knopf, 1946)
"There is a colored woman..." *Louisville Courier*, April 15, 1861, 1
"Voluntary Slavery," *Louisville Courier*, December 6, 1860, 1
"A Wealthy Colored Individual," *Louisville Courier*, March 9, 1861, 4
Wilson, C. D., "Negroes Who Owned Slaves," *Popular Science Monthly*, November 1912, 483-494
WPA Writers Project, *Virginia: A Guide to the Old Dominion* (New York: Oxford University Press, 1940)

Chapter 8

"Another Vallandigham Accident," *Louisville Courier-Journal*, June 29, 1871, 1
"Bloody Memories," *Louisville Courier-Journal*, December 5, 1870, 3
"Cincinnati," *Louisville Courier-Journal*, June 15, 1875, 1
"The *Cincinnati Commercial*..." *Louisville Courier-Journal*, July 20, 1871, 3
"Cogdell [*sic*] Doesn't Suicide," *Raleigh* [N.C.] *News and Observer*, June 11, 1902, 5
"Come See Me Die and Have Dinner," *Louisville Courier-Journal*, April 20, 1902, II, 4
"Died of Draft Fright," *Louisville Journal*, August 26, 1863, 1
Dr. Adonis, "A Sad Shooting Affair," *Louisville Journal*, February 15, 1864, 1
"Fatal Affray in Harrison County," *Louisville Journal*, July 12, 1864, 3
"A Fatal Spree Among Officers," *Louisville Journal*, March 28, 1868, 2
"His Name," *Louisville Journal*, June 30, 1865, 1
"In Hardin County..." *Louisville Courier-Journal*, October 1, 1868, 2
"Inquest No. 367," *Louisville Journal*, June 29, 1865, 1
Klement, F., *The Limits of Dissent* (Lexington: University Press of Kentucky, 1970)
"Mysterious Affair in Baltimore," *Louisville Journal*, January 14, 1865, 1
"Norfolk: The Great Trunk Tragedy," *Louisville Journal*, January 16, 1865, 1
"A Sad Occurrence," *Louisville Journal*. September 15, 1864, 1
"Shot by the Guard," *Louisville Journal*, December 6, 1864, 4
"Singular Death from Terror," *Louisville Journal*, July 20, 1865, 1
"Singular Suicide," *Louisville Journal*, April 13, 1866, 4
"The soldier that murdered himself..." *Louisville Journal*, June 29, 1865, 1
"While Gen. Paine lay wounded..." *Louisville Journal*, July 4, 1863, 1
"A young man..." *Louisville Journal*, August 27, 1865, 4

Chapter 9

"Anderson—His Burial..." *Louisville Journal*, November 9, 1864, 1
"Barbarous," *Louisville Journal*, August 13, 1863, 3
"The Battlefield a Fortnight after the Fight," *Louisville Courier*, August 30, 1861, 4
"The Battlefield of Bull Run," *Louisville Journal*, March 20, 1862, 1
"The battlefield of Franklin, TN..." *Louisville Journal*, May 22, 1866, 1
"Bill Anderson in Mortuis," *Louisville Journal*, November 9, 1864, 1
"Bill Stuart's Photograph," *Louisville Journal*, December 12, 1864, 1
Botkin, B. A., *A Civil War Treasury of Tales, Legends, and Folklore* (New York: Random House, 1960)
"Bowling Green," *Louisville Journal*, March 8, 1862, 1
"Bowling Green: The Fears of Pestilence," *Louisville Journal*, March 17, 1862, 2
"Burial of Soldiers," *Louisville Journal*, September 20, 1866, 3
"Burial of the Confederate Dead," *Louisville Journal*, April 30, 1867, 1
"Buried Alive," *Louisville Journal*, August 16, 1867, 2
"Camp Douglas," *Louisville Courier-Journal*, September 5, 1871, 3
"Cattle Plague," *Louisville Journal*, April 11, 1866, 1
"Corpse in a Carpetbag," *Louisville Journal*, December 5, 1865, 1
"Embalming," *Louisville Journal*, February 16, 1864, 4
Garrison, W., *Civil War Curiosities* (Nashville: Rutledge Hill Press, 1994); *A Treasury of Civil War Tales* (Nashville: Rutledge Hill Press, 1988)
"Horrible Fraud," *Louisville Journal*, December 30, 1867, 3
"Horrible Inhumanity," *Louisville Journal*, August 16, 1867, 2
"How Bodies Are Embalmed," *Louisville Journal*, November 13, 1864, 1
"How to Obtain the Bodies of Deceased Soldiers," *Louisville Journal*, October 12, 1865, 1
"The Human Jackals of Fort Harrison," *Richmond Dispatch*, April 10, 1869, 1
"Immediately in and around Bowling Green..." *Louisville Journal*, March 8, 1862, 2
"Injustice to the Dead," *Louisville Journal*, February 21, 1863, 3
"It is complained that the remains..." *Louisville Courier-Journal*, January 30, 1869, 2
"A late Richmond paper says..." *Louisville Journal*, July 4, 1864, 1
"A lawyer has been arrested..." *Louisville Journal*, April 24, 1863, 1
"The *Lebanon* [TN] *Herald* notices..." *Louisville Journal*, March 26, 1866, 3
Lochiel, "The Fight at Chaplin Hills," *Louisville Journal*, November 4, 1862, 3
"The *Mobile Advertiser* says..." *Louisville Journal*, January 30, 1864, 1
"Mutilation of Our Dead," *Louisville Journal*, March 22, 1862, 4
"The *Newnan* [GA] *Defender* says..." *Louisville Courier-Journal*, July 24, 1871, 2
"Perryville Battlefield," *Louisville Journal*, October 27, 1863, 2
"The *Petersburg Index* says..." *Louisville Journal*, September 15, 1866, 1
"The *Petersburg Index* says..." *Louisville Journal*, March 31, 1866, 3
"Playing Cards in a Cemetery Vault," *Louisville Courier-Journal*, January 20, 1884, 13
"Proposals for Burial of Deceased Soldiers," *Louisville Journal*, October 31, 1865, 2
"The Removal of the Dead," *Louisville Journal*, August 14, 1863, 1
"Shameful If True," *Louisville Journal*, March 28, 1867, 2
"A Shocking Statement," *Richmond Dispatch*. April 8, 1869, 1
"Singular Circumstance," *Louisville Journal*, March 14, 1864, 3
"A Singular Occurrence," *Louisville Journal*, December 1, 1864, 1
"A special to the *Cincinnati Gazette*..." *Louisville Journal*, March 20, 1862, 3
"The statement going the rounds..." *Louisville Courier-Journal*, September 2, 1869, 2
"Strange Incident," *Louisville Journal*, June 8, 1866, 3
Suhr, R., "The Dahlgren Affair," www.warfarehistorynetwork.com, 2024, warfarehistorynetwork.com/article/the-dahlgren-affair-kilpatrick-dahlgren-raid-on-richmond/

"There are 160,000 skeletons..." *Louisville Journal*, November 15, 1865, 4
"The Unburied Dead in the Wilderness," *Louisville Journal*, July 4, 1864, 1
"The Unknown Confederate Soldier," graymaine.org, www.graymaine.org/history/pages/the-unknown-confederate-soldier
"A visitor to the battlefield of Chickamauga..." *Louisville Journal*, July 18, 1865, 3
"Wirz," *Louisville Courier-Journal*, March 4, 1869, 3

Chapter 10

"Abraham Lincoln As a Reader and Conversationalist," *Louisville Journal*, February 26, 1867, 4
"Coincidence of Dreams," *Louisville Journal*, March 19, 1863, 4
"A Curious Incident," *Louisville Journal*, April 28, 1865, 1
"Joking and Suffering," *Louisville Journal*, January 28, 1864, 1
"Legislative Joking," *Louisville Courier*, February 26, 1861, 1
"President Lincoln Had a Presentiment of Death," *Louisville Journal*, May 2, 1865, 1
"A Prophecy in Jest," *Louisville Journal*, August 9, 1864, 1
"Reported Narrow Escape of the President," *Louisville Courier*, October 19, 1858, 1
"A Singular Prophecy," *Louisville Journal*, April 25, 1862, 1

Chapter 11

Bogar, T. A., *Backstage at the Lincoln Assassination* (Washington, D.C.: Regnery, 2013)
"Damages Recovered," *Louisville Courier*, April 11, 1861, 1
"Laura Keene has taken..." *Louisville Journal*, April 13, 1865, 3
"The suit of Miss Laura Keene..." *Louisville Journal*, December 14, 1865, 1
"Wood's Theater," *Louisville Journal*, May 15, 1865, 3
"Wood's Theater," *Louisville Journal*, May 19, 1865, 3
"Wood's Theater," *Louisville Journal*, October 23, 1865, 3
"Wood's Theater," *Louisville Journal*, October 25, 1865, 3

Chapter 12

"Business in the city..." *Louisville Journal*, April 25, 1865, 3
"Good places for seeing the procession..." *Louisville Journal*, May 9, 1865, 1
"Our Springfield Correspondence," *Louisville Journal*, May 7, 1865, 1
"The President After Death," *Louisville Journal*, April 21, 1865, 3
"Senator Douglas," *Louisville Journal*, June 4, 1868, 3
"To the Western Associated Press," *Louisville Journal*, April 21, 1865, 3
"To the Western Associated Press," *Louisville Journal*, April 26, 1865, 3

Chapter 13

"A boy has been arrested..." *Louisville Journal*, May 5, 1865, 3
Douglas, J., and Olshaker, M., *The Cases That Haunt Us* (N.Y.: Pocket Books, 2000)
"J.H. Blackburn..." *Louisville Journal*, May 8, 1865, 1
Sugden, P., *The Complete History of Jack the Ripper* (London: Robinson, 2002)
"Tumblety, alias Blackburn..." *Louisville Journal*, May 12, 1865, 1

Chapter 14

Bogar, T. A., *Backstage at the Lincoln Assassination* (Washington, D.C.: Regnery, 2013)
"The Custom House authorities..." *Louisville Journal*, November 30, 1865, 3
"The duty of placing..." *Louisville Journal*, August 9, 1865, 1
"The effects of the late..." *Louisville Journal*, October 15, 1865, 1
"It has been ascertained..." *Louisville Journal*, November 17, 1865, 3
"It is said the rascalities...." *Louisville Journal*, November 24, 1865, 3
"The name..." *Louisville Journal*, April 25, 1865, 1
"A New Proof of the Premeditation..." *Louisville Journal*, April 23, 1865, 3
"Officer Kenny..." *Louisville Journal*, May 15, 1866, 3
"On Wednesday night..." *Louisville Journal*, April 24, 1865, 1
"One hundred dollars were offered..." *Louisville Journal*, July 17, 1865, 3
"Preston King and Mrs. Surratt," *Louisville Journal*, July 30, 1867, 4
"Preston King's Body Recovered," *Louisville Journal*, May 19, 1866, 1
"The remains of Preston King..." *Louisville Journal*, May 15, 1866, 3
"A reward of $500..." *Louisville Journal*, November 17, 1865, 3
"The room occupied..." *Louisville Journal*, January 26, 1867, 1
"A rumor comes from Washington..." *Louisville Journal*, November 30, 1865, 1
"The Trial and Execution," *Louisville Journal*, July 15, 1865, 1
"To the Associated Press," *Louisville Journal*, November 15, 1865, 3
"The unfortunate death of Preston King..." *Louisville Journal*, November 16, 1865, 1
"A well known citizen of Baltimore..." *Louisville Journal*, April 29, 1865, 3

Chapter 15

"Bombshell, Relic of Civil War, Is Found," *Louisville Courier-Journal*, March 24, 1917, 9
"Cannon Ball Found," *Louisville Courier-Journal*, May 15, 1922, 6
"A Cannon Ball in a Tree," *Louisville Courier-Journal*, January 6, 1892, 7
"A dreadful incident..." *Louisville Courier-Journal*, July 25, 1870, 2
"An explosion took place..." *Louisville Journal*, January 31, 1867, 2
"A forgotten torpedo..." *Louisville Journal*, August 25, 1866, 4
"Hiram Reeves..." *Louisville Journal*, December 16, 1868, 2
Mustermann, E., "Civil War Cannonball Exploded and Killed 140 Years After It Was Fired," War History Online, April 4, 2020, www.warhistoryonline.com/news/civil-war-2.html
"A Negro boy..." *Louisville Journal*, June 12, 1866, 1
"Old War Shells Are Dangerous," *Louisville Courier-Journal*, January 8, 1911, II, 4
"Pistol Long Buried Still Carries Death," *Louisville Courier-Journal*, March 8, 1907, 1
"Success with a Vengeance," *Louisville Courier-Journal*, April 1, 1892, 2
"There is said to be..." *Louisville Courier-Journal*, November 9, 1873, 1
"Three Charleston..." *Louisville Journal*, February 9, 1867, 2
"A torpedo..." *Louisville Journal*, June 14, 1866, 1

Chapter 16

"Amusing Incident," *Louisville Journal*, August 31, 1864, 1
Barnes, Stacy, email to author, July 9, 2021
"A Bony Mystery Revealed," *Louisville Courier-Journal*, April 16, 1891, 1
"The Charleston..." *Louisville Journal*, March 7, 1867, 3

"Columbus, Ga," *Louisville Courier-Journal*, December 18, 1873, 2
"The correspondent..." *Louisville Journal*, February 4, 1864, 1
"'Dead Head' Extraordinary," *Louisville Journal*, August 24, 1866, 1
"A Detroit druggist..." *Louisville Courier-Journal*, June 12, 1871, 3
"Digs Up Skeleton of Human Being," *Louisville Courier-Journal*, April 16, 1907, 1
"Epitaph Lauds Scalding of Soldiers," *Louisville Courier-Journal*, March 12, 1939, I, 10
"A Faithful Dog," *Louisville Journal*, December 3, 1862, 1
"The Field of Antietam," *Louisville Journal*, July 30, 1863, 1
"A Fish Story," *Louisville Journal*, May 25, 1868, 4
"The *Fredericksburg* [VA] *News* says..." *Louisville Courier-Journal*, July 15, 1871, 2
"Ghastly Reminder," *Louisville Courier-Journal*, September 17, 1916, II, 6
"Ghost or Goblin," *Louisville Journal*, July 25, 1868, 1
"A Ghostly Tenant," *Louisville Times*, November 28, 1892
"A Haunted House," *Louisville Courier-Journal*, May 2, 1885, 2
"It is suggested by a Richmond paper..." *Louisville Journal*, April 5, 1866, 3
"Keeps 'Hardtack' 50 Years," *Louisville Courier-Journal*, June 24, 1916, 3
"Long-Haired Vet Dies," *Louisville Courier-Journal*, March 12, 1937, III, 1
"Major Thomas G. Jones..." *Louisville Courier-Journal*, May 3, 1877, 2
"The *Mobile Advertiser* says..." *Louisville Journal*, August 27, 1866, 3
"More Tales Recalled by Discovery..." *Louisville Courier-Journal*, July 31, 1904, III, 7
"Near Wadesboro..." *Louisville Journal*, April 14, 1866, 3
"New Military Cemetery at Vicksburg," *Louisville Journal*, April 6, 1867, 3
"On the Death of Zollicoffer," *Louisville Journal*, February 10, 1862, 3
"Opelousas [LA] ..." *Louisville Courier-Journal*, March 20, 1874, 2
"A package which..." *Louisville Courier-Journal*, December 14, 1883, 7
"Partially Identify Body of Confederate," *Louisville Courier-Journal*, October 28, 1909, 8
"The Remains of a Confederate Soldier," *Louisville Journal*, May 18, 1866, 4
"Richmond *Herald*," *Louisville Courier-Journal*, April 22, 1880, 2
"Says Master Buried $11,000 in Gold," *Louisville Courier-Journal*, July 22, 1905, 3
"Singular Circumstances," *Louisville Journal*, May 27, 1864, 1
"Skeleton of Unknown Confederate Soldier," *Louisville Courier-Journal*, August 25, 1901, I, 5
"A Soldier's Skeleton," *Louisville Courier-Journal*, January 5, 1892, 5
"A Spiritualistic paper..." *Louisville Journal*, August 17, 1866, 1
"A Strange Discovery," *Louisville Journal*, August 31, 1866, 1
"Terra Cotta Coffin Unearthed," *Louisville Courier-Journal*, September 3, 1909, 5
"Treasure Found Buried in Mysterious Graves," *Louisville Courier-Journal*, November 20, 1901, 6
"Two Ghost Stories," *Louisville Courier-Journal*, November 15, 1871, 2

Chapter 17

"About Holt Collier," *Louisville Courier-Journal,* November 23, 1902, I, 10
Anderson, T. F., "The Cherokee Indians," *Louisville Courier-Journal,* November 19, 1877, 3
Austerman, W. R., "The Black Confederates," in *Forgotten Confederates: An Anthology About Black Southerners*, eds. Charles Kelly Barrow, J. H. Segars, and R. B. Rosenburg, *Journal of Confederate History Studies, Vol. XIV* (Atlanta: Southern Heritage Press, 1995)
Bergeron, Jr., A. W., "Free Men of Color in Grey," *Civil War History* 32.3 (1986), 247-255
"The bill authorizing the impressment..." *Louisville Journal,* February 18, 1863, 1
"Black Confederate Soldier Honored," *Atlanta Journal-Constitution*, June 20, 1999, M5

Cartwright, T. Y., "Better Confederates Did Not Live," in *Black Southerners in Gray: Essays in Afro-Americans in Confederate Armies*, ed. Richard Rollins, *Journal of Confederate History Studies, Vol. XI* (Murfreesboro, TN.: Southern Heritage Press, 1994)
"Comrade Jerry," *Louisville Courier-Journal,* June 3, 1900, II, 7
"Confederates Do Honor to Ante-Bellum Negro," *Louisville Courier-Journal,* October 13, 1905, 1
Cotton, G., "Local Blacks Given Pensions for Service to the Confederacy," *Vicksburg* [MS] *Sunday Post*, September 23, 1984, D4
"David J. Deas..." *Louisville Courier-Journal,* January 16, 1872, 2
"Draws Confederate Pension and Wears Southern Cross of Honor," *Louisville Courier-Journal,* March 18, 1917, II, 1
"Ex-Negro Slave, Member of CSA Army, is Dead," *Louisville Courier-Journal,* March 19, 1922, IV, 12
"A Former Slave Gives $1,000 to Aid Town," *Louisville Courier-Journal,* July 17, 1901, 4
"From Fortress Monroe: The Late Skirmish," *New York Tribune,* December 25, 1861, 5
"From Fortress Monroe: The Skirmish," *New York Tribune,* December 26, 1861, 5
Garrison, W., *Civil War Curiosities* (Nashville: Rutledge Hill Press, 1994); *More Civil War Curiosities* (Nashville, TN: Rutledge Hill Press, 1995)
"Gen. Wheeler's Bodyguard," *Louisville Courier-Journal,* October 8, 1923, 6
"Gives $1,000," *Louisville Courier-Journal,* January 30, 1901, 2
"Grizzled Old Negro Wishes for Old Days..." *Louisville Courier-Journal,* June 15, 1905, 5
"The guerrilla Richardson..." *Louisville Journal,* August 12, 1863, 3
Harper, C. W., "Black Loyalty Under the Confederacy," in *Forgotten Confederates: An Anthology About Black Southerners*, eds. Charles Kelly Barrow, J. H. Segars, and R. B. Rosenburg, *Journal of Confederate History Studies, Vol. XIV* (Atlanta: Southern Heritage Press, 1995)
Harrison, J. L., "A Tribute to Loyal Confederates," in *Forgotten Confederates: An Anthology About Black Southerners*, eds. Charles Kelly Barrow, J. H. Segars, and R. B. Rosenburg, *Journal of Confederate History Studies, Vol. XIV* (Atlanta: Southern Heritage Press, 1995)
"The impressment of able-bodied Negroes..." *Louisville Journal,* February 10, 1864, 1
"In Abolitionist Indiana," *Louisville Courier-Journal,* March 8, 1891, 5
Jordan, Jr., E. L., "Different Drummers: Black Virginians as Confederate Loyalists," in *Black Southerners in Gray: Essays in Afro-Americans in Confederate Armies*, ed. Richard Rollins, *Journal of Confederate History Studies, Vol. XI* (Murfreesboro, TN: Southern Heritage Press, 1994)
Kennedy, J. R., and Kennedy, W. D., *The South Was Right!* (Gretna, LA: Pelican Publishing Co., 1996)
Loewen, J. W., *Lies Across America* (New York: New Press, 1999)
Lunsford, P. C., "The Forgotten Confederates," in *Forgotten Confederates: An Anthology About Black Southerners*, eds. Charles Kelly Barrow, J. H. Segars, and R. B. Rosenburg, *Journal of Confederate History Studies, Vol. XIV* (Atlanta: Southern Heritage Press, 1995)
"The Mayor of Charleston..." *Louisville Journal,* July 25, 1863, 1
"Monument to Indians Who Fought for the Confederacy," *Louisville Courier-Journal,* August 4, 1900, 3
"A Negro Confederate," *Louisville Courier-Journal,* August 9, 1900, 3
"Negro Confederate Soldier Dies," *Louisville Courier-Journal,* September 9, 1910, 3
"Negro Confederate Veteran" *Louisville Courier-Journal,* December 13, 1911, 6
"Negroes in the Creek Nation" *Louisville Courier-Journal,* February 21, 1901, 3
"Old Document Shows Indians Freed Slaves," *Louisville Courier-Journal,* December 26, 1932, 19
"On the following day..." *Louisville Journal,* February 12, 1864, 1
"Origin of Arming Negroes," *Louisville Journal,* June 2, 1863, 1
"Paducah *Kentuckian*..." *Louisville Courier-Journal,* June 3, 1874, 2
Potter, G., "Catholicism in the Old South," Catholicism.org, May 16, 2005, www.catholicism.org/catholicism-south.html

"A Proposition to Arm Negroes," *Louisville Journal,* June 4, 1862, 4
"The Question Stated," *New York Tribune,* December 26, 1861, 4
"A Real Christmas Story," editorial, *Louisville Courier-Journal,* December 25, 1919, 6
"Rebel [Negroes]," *Louisville Journal,* May 19, 1863, 1
Rollins, R., "Black Confederates at Gettysburg," in *Black Southerners in Gray: Essays in Afro-Americans in Confederate Armies*, ed. Richard Rollins, *Journal of Confederate History Studies, Vol. XI* (Murfreesboro, TN: Southern Heritage Press, 1994); "Black Southerners in Gray," in *Black Southerners in Gray: Essays in Afro Americans in Confederate Armies*, ed. Richard Rollins, *Journal of Confederate History Studies, Vol. XI* (Murfreesboro, TN: Southern Heritage Press, 1994); "Servants and Soldiers," in *Black Southerners in Gray: Essays in Afro-Americans in Confederate Armies*, ed. Richard Rollins, *Journal of Confederate History Studies, Vol. XI* (Murfreesboro, TN: Southern Heritage Press, 1994)
Segars, J. H., "Black Southerners in Gray?" in *Forgotten Confederates: An Anthology About Black Southerners*, eds. Charles Kelly Barrow, J. H. Segars, and R. B. Rosenburg, *Journal of Confederate History Studies, Vol. XIV* (Atlanta: Southern Heritage Press, 1995)
Shenkman, R., and Reiger, K., *One Night Stands with American History* (New York: Quill, 1982)
"Slavery Not Extinct," *Philadelphia Press*, May 15, 1883, 5
"Slavery in Florida," *Louisville Courier-Journal,* January 5, 1890, 6
Sons of Confederate Veterans, "Black History Month: Black Confederate Heritage," SonsofConfederateVeterans.org, August 2019, scv.org/wp-content/uploads/2019/08/blackhistory-1.pdf
Starkey, M. L., *The Cherokee Nation* (New York: Knopf, 1946)
Thompson, J., "Benavides, Refugio," Handbook of Texas Online, October 25, 2021, www.tshaonline.org/handbook/entries/benavides-refugio
"Treachery of a Negro Guide," *Louisville Journal,* March 15, 1864, 1
Wiley, B. I., *The Life of Johnny Reb* (Baton Rouge: Louisiana State University Press, 1978. Reprint of 1943 edition)
Wilson, C. D., "Negroes Who Owned Slaves," *Popular Science Monthly*, November 1912, 483-494
Young, R., "Black Confederates in Lincoln County, North Carolina," in *Black Southerners in Gray: Essays in Afro-Americans in Confederate Armies*, ed. Richard Rollins, *Journal of Confederate History Studies, Vol. XI* (Murfreesboro, TN.: Southern Heritage Press, 1994)

Chapter 18

"Acquitted of Desecrating Graves," *Louisville Courier-Journal,* September 10, 1898, 10
"Camp Douglas," *Louisville Courier-Journal,* September 5, 1871, 3
"A Corporal's Evidence," *Louisville Courier-Journal,* August 17, 1898, 4
"Court-Martial Trial," *Louisville Courier-Journal,* August 12, 1898, 2
"Court-Martial Trial," *Louisville Courier-Journal,* August 16, 1898, 3
"Desecrating Soldiers' Graves," *Louisville Courier-Journal,* May 1, 1895, 6
"Duncan is Guilty," *Louisville Courier-Journal,* August 30, 1898, 4
"Evidence All Heard," *Louisville Courier-Journal,* August 19, 1898, 2
"The Grave-Robbing Case," *Louisville Courier-Journal,* August 24, 1898, 5
"A profound feeling of horror..." *Louisville Journal,* November 12, 1863, 1
"Resurrectionists," *Louisville Journal,* December 1, 1864, 1
Woolley, B., "A Mountain Mystery and An Empty Grave," *Louisville Courier-Journal*, April 7, 1976, D5

Chapter 19

"An Answer Expected," *Louisville Journal*, May 26, 1840, 2
"The *Ashland Journal...*" *Louisville Courier-Journal,* May 8, 1871, 2
"Change of Circumstances," *Louisville Courier,* January 19, 1858, 1
"Criminal Court," *Louisville Courier,* October 30, 1858, 1
"The Eagle's Last Flight," *Louisville Courier,* August 31, 1859, 1
"The editor of the *St. Louis Republican...*" *Louisville Journal*, March 10, 1840, 2
"An Evansville man..." *Louisville Courier-Journal,* March 31, 1875, 3
"Fate of a Vagrant," *Louisville Courier-Journal*, March 3, 1887, 2
"Four Woman and One Man to Be Sold..." *Louisville Courier,* October 22, 1858, 1
"Georgetown's Negro Vagrants," *Louisville Courier-Journal,* February 21, 1895, 4
"Great Fall in Flesh," *Louisville Courier-Journal,* December 15, 1880, 3
"*Henderson* [KY] *Reporter*," *Louisville Courier-Journal,* March 27, 1875, 2
"Henry E. Dodson..." *Louisville Courier-Journal*, February 24, 1887, 1
"Human Being's Price is One Dollar," *Louisville Courier-Journal,* December 4, 1906, 2
"In Kentucky a man..." *Louisville Courier-Journal,* March 13, 1887, 12
"Kentucky News," *Louisville Courier-Journal,* January 9, 1885, 7
"A Know-Nothing Vagrant," *Louisville Courier,* November 17, 1855, 2
"Life's Changes," *Louisville Courier,* March 19, 1858, 1
"Magnolia [N.C.]," *Louisville Courier-Journal,* April 24, 1876, 2
"Matters in Kentucky," *Louisville Courier-Journal,* November 2, 1897, 4
"Mean Specimens," *Louisville Courier,* August 6, 1859, 1
"Negro Farmer Purchases a Black Brother..." *Louisville Courier-Journal,* September 7, 1902, III, 1
"A Negro man was sold at auction..." *Louisville Courier-Journal,* July 16, 1869, 2
"Negro Vagrant Will Be Offered for Sale..." *Louisville Courier-Journal,* September 5, 1902, 1
"Odds and Ends of State News," *Louisville Courier-Journal,* March 21, 1895, 4
"Once More," *Louisville Courier,* January 12, 1858, 2
"Pauper Auctions," *Louisville Courier,* March 17, 1853, 2
"A Pauper Bids Herself In," *Louisville Courier-Journal,* January 11, 1899, 4
"*Petersburg* [VA] *Index*," *Louisville Courier-Journal,* January 5, 1875, 2
"Police Court," *Louisville Courier,* January 15, 1858, 1
"Police Court," *Louisville Courier,* May 14, 1860, 1
"Price of a White Man," *Louisville Journal*, May 13, 1857, 3
"*Richmond* [KY] *Register*," *Louisville Courier-Journal,* September 30, 1876, 2
"The Sale of a Vagrant," *Louisville Courier-Journal,* June 15, 1882, 6
"The Sale of Vagrants," *Louisville Courier-Journal,* February 21, 1895, 4
"Selling White Men," *Louisville Journal*, June 10, 1843, 2
"Sets Aside Sale of White Man," *Louisville Courier-Journal,* December 10, 1906, 1
"Shelbyville," *Louisville Courier-Journal,* October 4, 1902, 8
"Slavery as a Punishment for Crime," *Louisville Courier-Journal,* July 12, 1882, 2
"Taylorsville Vagrant Sold into Servitude," *Louisville Courier-Journal,* August 7, 1901, 1
"The Tables Turned," *Niles' Register*, December 1, 1821, Vol. 21, 214
"Their Services of Little Value," *Louisville Courier-Journal,* February 10, 1895, 3
"Two Negro Women Sell For $5 Apiece," *Louisville Courier-Journal,* November 29, 1902, I, 1
"Negroes Sold at Auction," *Louisville Courier-Journal,* March 30, 1892, 1
"Two White Women Sold..." *Louisville Courier-Journal,* August 13, 1875, 3
"The Vagrancy Law," *Louisville Courier-Journal,* July 13, 1900, 4
"Vagrancy Not a Crime," *Louisville Courier-Journal,* August 28, 1895, 1
"A Vagrant Sold," *Louisville Courier-Journal,* August 5, 1896, 5
"Vagrant Question," *Louisville Courier,* October 28, 1858, 1

"Vagrant Question," *Louisville Courier,* October 30, 1858, 1
"We copy the following..." *Louisville Journal*, April 1, 1837, 2
"Whipping and Selling Poor White Men..." *Louisville Courier,* June 29, 1848, 3
"A white female pauper..." *Louisville Courier-Journal,* January 28, 1869, 2
"White Man Sold," *Louisville Courier,* November 15, 1858, 1
"A white man was sold for vagrancy..." *Louisville Courier,* June 13, 1853, 2
"Will Sell White Man," *Louisville Courier-Journal,* November 26, 1906, 4
"A Woman to be Sold for Vagrancy," *Louisville Courier-Journal,* June 4, 1887, 2
"Young White Man Sold for Vagrancy," *Louisville Courier-Journal,* April 13, 1903, 6

Chapter 20

"American Slavery," *Louisville Courier-Journal*, December 25, 1889, 2
"A Diary of Horror," *Louisville Courier-Journal*, February 24, 1896, 1
Garrison, W., *More Civil War Curiosities* (Nashville: Rutledge Hill Press, 1995)
"Hon. Henry J. Raymond..." *Louisville Journal*, February 3, 1863, 1
"Just Learned of Negro Emancipation," *Louisville Courier-Journal*, February 9, 1887, 2
"The New Bern *Republican*..." *Louisville Courier-Journal*, June 30, 1871, 2
"An Old Father's Love," *Louisville Courier-Journal*, October 2, 1893, 2
"Peculiar Claim Made by Civil War Veteran," *Louisville Courier-Journal*, November 5, 1911, II, 4
"Pennsylvania as a Slave State," *Louisville Courier-Journal*, September 16, 1875, 1
"A Remarkable Story," *Louisville Journal*, March 10, 1868, 1
"Rip Van Winkle has turned up..." *Louisville Courier-Journal*, June 26, 1869, 3
"Romantic History and Death of a Brooklyn Girl," *Louisville Journal*, March 1, 1864, 4
"A Romantic Incident," *Louisville Journal*, February 24, 1864, 1
"Skeleton in a Cave," *Louisville Courier-Journal*, May 28, 1890, 2
"Slave Just Freed," *Indianapolis Journal*, September 15, 1893, 4
"A Wanderer for Years," *Pittsburgh Post*, September 21, 1891, 4

Chapter 21

"Death Brings End to Vigil of Love," *Louisville Courier-Journal*, April 12, 1931, I, 10
"Happy Ending to Shattered Romance," *Louisville Courier-Journal*, September 2, 1910, 3
"Melancholy Suicide," *Louisville Courier*, November 12, 1861, 4
"The *Norfolk Virginian* relates..." *Louisville Courier-Journal*, July 19, 1871, 2
"A Romance of Slavery Days," *Louisville Courier-Journal*, January 19, 1884, 4
"Soldier's Lone Grave," *Louisville Courier-Journal*, January 9, 1901, 5
"We remember at the Battle of the Wilderness..." *Louisville Journal*, April 25, 1866, 4